InterActions
small group series

Developing
Deeper
Devotion
to Christ

COMMITMENT

Interactions Small Group Series

InterActions
small group series

Developing
Deeper
Devotion
to Christ

COMMITMENT

BILL HYBELS

WITH KEVIN AND SHERRY HARNEY

ZONDERVAN™

GRAND RAPIDS, MICHIGAN 49530 USA

WILLOW
Willow Creek Resources

We want to hear from you. Please send your comments about this book to us in care of zreview@zondervan.com. Thank you.

ZONDERVAN™

Commitment
Copyright © 1996 by Willow Creek Association

Requests for information should be addressed to:

Zondervan, *Grand Rapids, Michigan 49530*

ISBN-10: 0-310-26595-9
ISBN-13: 978-0-310-26595-5

Interior design by Rick Devon and Michelle Espinoza

Printed in the United States of America

05 06 07 08 09 10 11 12 /❖ DCI/ 10 9 8 7 6 5 4 3 2 1

CONTENTS

INTERACTIONS

In 1992, Willow Creek Community Church, in partnership with Zondervan and the Willow Creek Association, released a curriculum for small groups entitled the Walking with God series. In just three years, almost a half million copies of these small group study guides were being used in churches around the world. The phenomenal response to this curriculum affirmed the need for relevant and biblical small group materials.

At the writing of this curriculum, there are nearly 3,000 small groups meeting regularly within the structure of Willow Creek Community Church. We believe this number will increase as we continue to place a central value on small groups. Many other churches throughout the world are growing in their commitment to small group ministries as well, so the need for resources is increasing.

In response to this great need, the Interactions small group series has been developed. Willow Creek Association and Zondervan have joined together to create a whole new approach to small group materials. These discussion guides are meant to challenge group members to a deeper level of sharing, to create lines of accountability, to move followers of Christ into action, and to help group members become fully devoted followers of Christ.

SUGGESTIONS FOR INDIVIDUAL STUDY

1. Begin each session with prayer. Ask God to help you understand the passage and to apply it to your life.
2. A good modern translation, such as the New International Version, the New American Standard Bible, or the New Revised Standard Version, will give you the most help. Questions in this guide are based on the New International Version.
3. Read and reread the passage(s). You must know what the passage says before you can understand what it means and how it applies to you.
4. Write your answers in the spaces provided in the study guide. This will help you to express clearly your understanding of the passage.

5. Keep a Bible dictionary handy. Use it to look up unfamiliar words, names, or places.

Suggestions for Group Study

1. Come to the session prepared. Careful preparation will greatly enrich your time in group discussion.
2. Be willing to join in the discussion. The leader of the group will not be lecturing, but will encourage people to discuss what they have learned in the passage. Plan to share what God has taught you in your individual study.
3. Stick to the passage being studied. Base your answers on the verses being discussed rather than on outside authorities such as commentaries or your favorite author or speaker.
4. Try to be sensitive to the other members of the group. Listen attentively when they speak, and be affirming whenever you can. This will encourage more hesitant members of the group to participate.
5. Be careful not to dominate the discussion. By all means participate! But allow others to have equal time.
6. If you are the discussion leader, you will find additional suggestions and helpful ideas in the leader's notes.

Additional Resources and Teaching Materials

At the end of this study guide you will find a collection of resources and teaching materials to help you in your growth as a follower of Christ. You will also find resources that will help your church develop and build fully devoted followers of Christ.

Introduction: Developing Deeper Devotion to Christ

Remember that time you beat your best friend at tennis and found yourself thinking, *Hey, I'm pretty good!* Then you went to a professional tournament and it looked like the balls were coming out of shoulder-mounted rocket launchers. You said to yourself, *If I step on that court with those pros, I'm likely to get hurt. They are out of my league."*

Or maybe you're a weekend hacker at golf. Occasionally you'll hit two or three drives right down the middle of the fairway and start feeling pretty good about your game. You say to yourself, *Tiger, eat your heart out!* Then you watch a professional tournament and you see a real pro smack a ball three hundred yards, straight as an arrow. At those moments you have to be honest and say to yourself, *These players are way out of my league.*

What does it feel like to be "out of your league?" You might feel a little small or like you might just as well quit. All of us feel like giving up at some point in our lives. No matter how committed we are, we'll never be as good as the superstars and pros.

In the first century A.D., there existed a small group of men called Scribes and Pharisees who were widely revered as the religious elite. The unchallenged superstars of spirituality, they raised religious fervor to an art form. They put the bar of spiritual expectations so high that the average man or woman would say of them, "These guys are out of my league. I could never compete in religion against them. I would have to quit my job and work at religion twenty-four hours a day to obey all the rules they have put into effect. There are too many hoops to jump through. The bar is so high I feel like quitting rather than competing at the level they have set."

Against this cultural backdrop enters Jesus—the mystery man of the first century. Thirty years old and physically indistinguishable from other guys His age, He comes from a small town, from a common family, but soon after He arrives strange things start to happen. One time, He was in a large public gathering listening to a prophet named John the Baptist. When John saw Jesus at the edge of the crowd, he cried out, "Look everybody. Look at this man. He's the Lamb of God who came to earth to take away the sins of the world. Look everybody, there's God's Son in human flesh." You better believe that sent a ripple through the crowd.

Shortly thereafter, Jesus was baptized. When He came out of the water, the clouds parted and a voice from heaven thundered, "This is My Son, and I'm pleased with Him. I love Him." That certainly raised a few eyebrows.

A short time later, Jesus started going around doing miracles and healings. Matthew 4:24 tells us He healed every kind of sickness and disease. The lame walked, the blind saw, the deaf heard. Lepers had new skin. Jesus' miracles sent huge tidal waves of response through the area. There was more controversy and curiosity about Jesus of Nazareth than anybody walking the planet at that time.

In this atmosphere, Jesus climbed a hillside and sat down to teach. All the people were eager to hear what he had to say. They were disillusioned by the legalistic religion of the Pharisees, but they still wanted to be committed to God. Jesus' high-powered message that day, now called "The Sermon on the Mount," is considered by many to be the greatest sermon in history.

In this series of interactions, we will explore six different passages from this famous sermon. Along the way, we will discover that the message Jesus preached on that hillside is just as powerful and life-changing today as it was two thousand years ago.

Bill Hybels

HANG ON FOR HEAVEN

THE BIG PICTURE

Have you ever heard someone use the expression, "I thought I'd died and gone to heaven?" A business woman from Chicago goes on a business trip to Phoenix in February. She is looking forward to getting there so she can get some sun between business meetings. Her single room is unavailable so they have to upgrade her to a luxury suite with a sun-drenched balcony overlooking the pool. The next day her meetings are canceled and she is free to spend the whole day relaxing. She phones a friend and says, "I feel like I've died and gone to heaven."

After a round of golf, a guy in a bar "tips a few" and begins to tell about his putt on the eighteenth green. He recounts how he hit his ball with a perfect stroke, how it took two huge breaks, going up a hill and then down and finally rolled straight into the heart of the cup. He finishes by saying, "I won a ten-dollar bet and I thought I'd died and gone to heaven."

A fan at a Bulls' basketball game gets to take a shot from half court. He's told, "If you make this shot, we'll give you a million bucks." He makes it! When he tells that story, he probably says "and when that ball went through the hoop, I thought I'd died and gone to heaven."

When we use that expression, we're trying to explain an experience that resulted in a euphoria that goes beyond description. Sometimes I want to ask people, "Do you know where that expression originated? Do you know the origin of the concept of heaven?" It was not from Greek mythology or Persian fantasy. It's not a Shakespearean concept. It is not simply an invention of the English language to express great joy. I think a lot of people use the expression and don't even realize that the concept of heaven is uniquely biblical. It comes right out of the teachings of Jesus. And brace yourselves. Jesus taught about heaven and made it sound as real as earth. He really believed in such a place and spent a lot of time and energy convincing other people that heaven was real.

A WIDE ANGLE VIEW

1 Describe your image of heaven when you were a child.

What is your image of heaven now?

A BIBLICAL PORTRAIT

Read Matthew 5:10–12

2 How do you feel when you hear the statement, "Blessed are those who are persecuted because of righteousness . . ."? Blessed means "truly happy." How can the persecuted be truly happy?

What kind of persecution do you think Jesus was talking about?

3 Jesus assures His followers that the persecutions and sufferings of this life can't compare with the rewards and joys of heaven. How does the hope of heaven impact the way you live your life today?

SHARPENING THE FOCUS

4 Jesus gives His followers a sobering and tough piece of information when He tells them that they will pay a price for following Him. In light of the world we live in, how are followers of Christ persecuted today?

Read Snapshot "Moral Irritations"

MORAL IRRITATIONS

One reason Christ followers will take hits in this world is because they unwittingly become moral irritations to family, friends and colleagues when they follow Christ diligently. It's like the gangly fourth grade girl in my elementary school. Her name was Ardith. We froze her out of our social circle for the simple reason that her grades broke the curve for the rest of us who weren't as diligent with our studies. She would get an "A" on a test and mess up the curve for all the rest of us. We just wanted to say, "Hey, Ardith, would you chill out a little bit on the grades thing? You're making the rest of us look really bad." She was becoming an academic irritation to the rest of us. This very dynamic often unfolds in the relational network of Christ followers who are just trying to do their best in leading God-honoring lives. However, like Ardith, we can become an irritation when our lives look different than the lives of those who don't follow Christ.

5 In what ways might fully committed followers of Christ be a moral irritation in today's world?

- In the marketplace

- In their homes

- In friendships with seekers

- In school settings

How have you experienced this in your life?

Read Snapshot "Stand Firm and Smile"

STAND FIRM AND SMILE

What is a Christ follower to do when persecution comes? Jesus gives us some answers in this passage. When you follow Christ and model His value system, you're on a collision course with people. He says to do two things. First, *stand firm*. Don't run scared. Don't cave in. Don't shrink back. Stand firm. Second, *smile on the inside*. Even though you are taking a beating on the outside, smile on the inside. Actually, His phrase is "Rejoice and be glad." Smile on the inside, knowing why you are smiling. It's not because it feels good to be beat up. It's because you know that Christ is going to make it worthwhile some day in heaven. Heaven will make our battle scars on earth worth it many times over. Stand firm and smile, knowing that "great is your reward in heaven."

6 What can you do to stand firm even when persecution comes?

Read Snapshot "What If?"

WHAT IF?

Have you ever been on a flight and heard a flight attendant use the phrase "In the unlikely event of a water landing, your seat cushion can be used as a flotation device"? I heard that on a flight from Atlanta to Chicago. Think about it. There is not a great chance of ever needing a flotation device on a flight between those two inland cities.

However, there is another "What if" situation we should all be ready for. I want to ask, "In the unlikely event that you end up living in a culture where there is overt hostility and persecution, are you certain how you would respond?"

Let's be honest, for most people reading these words, things are pretty comfortable right now. But there are places right now where people gather to worship, to listen to teaching from the Bible, and to pray, and they do so at the risk of imprisonment and death. Now, in the unlikely event that human history were to take a drastic change and we were to be in a culture like that, and the threat of imprisonment was possible because you were worshiping with other Christ followers, would you still be committed to gather for worship?

What are some outward signs that a Christ follower is smiling on the inside?

7 How do you think you would respond to a life-threatening, full-scale persecution of Christians?

What can you do to prepare yourself to be able to stand for Jesus and hang on for heaven no matter what the cost?

8 What can the members of your small group do to help you grow in you commitment to live for Jesus, no matter what they face?

PUTTING YOURSELF IN THE PICTURE

HONEST REFLECTION: AM I AN IRRITATION?

Jesus never asked us to be needlessly irritating. However, He was clear that fully devoted followers will sometimes become moral irritations by virtue of their unwavering commitment to follow Him no matter what the cost. Take time in the coming days to reflect on your own life.

- Are there ways in which you are *needlessly* irritating others that might drive those who are seekers away from Christ? If so, commit yourself to change these behaviors and practices. Also, ask a friend in your small group to keep you accountable as you learn to stop doing things that could push people away from Jesus.
- Are there ways you are an irritation because you have committed yourself to an uncompromising lifestyle of seeking Jesus? If so, thank God for bringing you so far that your life is being transformed and making an impact on the world around you.

Discuss how you can support one another when you take one on the chin for being a moral irritation.

COMMIT TO MEMORIZING SCRIPTURE

Blessed are those who are persecuted because of righteousness, for theirs is the kingdom of heaven (Matt. 5:10).

DEVELOPING A HEART OF FAITH

REFLECTIONS FROM SESSION 1

1. If you memorized and meditated on Matthew 5:10, how has the truth of this passage inspired you to hang on for heaven?
2. If you identified an area in your life where you might be causing needless irritation, what are you doing to change your actions or patterns?

THE BIG PICTURE

One afternoon a friend and I were going to go running. He was a little late getting to my house, so while I waited I took out a basketball and started shooting some hoops in front of my house.

I don't mean to brag, but I got in the zone. I was shooting free throws, and one after another was going in. When my friend showed up, he just stood under the hoop and fed me the ball. I was hitting so many, he said, "Well, let's see how many you can do in a row." One, two, three, four, five, six. He said, "You're going for the world record." I said, "Maybe." And I proceeded to miss the very next shot.

Out of curiosity, the next day I asked my secretary to look up what the Guiness world record was for consecutive free throws. What do you think it is? What is the most free throws any human being has made without missing one? Would you guess seventy? Eighty? Seven hundred? Eight hundred? If you guessed any of these numbers, you're not even close! The world record for most consecutive free throws is 2,036.

Amazing! So the next time you make a thousand free throws in a row, realize you are less than halfway to the world record.

Try to imagine if God set the standard for entering heaven on our ability to make free throws. What if God said, "I know the Guiness world record is 2,036, but the standard I am setting for consecutive free throws is ten thousand." What would you say? How would you respond? We would all probably say, "You've got to be kidding. The world record is 2,036 and You're going to bump it up five times? Ten thousand! Forget it. There is no possible way."

A WIDE ANGLE VIEW

1 How would you feel toward God if He set an unreachable standard as the prerequisite for entering heaven?

How would you respond if someone came to you and asked, "What must I do to enter heaven?"

A BIBLICAL PORTRAIT

Read Matthew 5:17–20

2 Jesus said, "Do not think that I have come to abolish the Law or the Prophets; I have not come to abolish them but to fulfill them." What does He mean by "the Law or the Prophets," and how has Jesus fulfilled the Law and the Prophets?

3 Jesus appears to set an unreachable standard when He says, "Unless your righteousness surpasses that of the Pharisees and the teachers of the law, you will certainly not enter the kingdom of heaven." How can our righteousness actually go beyond that of the religious leaders of Jesus' day?

SHARPENING THE FOCUS

Read Snapshot "A Story of a Hardhead"

A STORY OF A HARDHEAD

In Luke 7 there's a story about a theology professor named Simon. Simon can't wait to have a one-on-one, intellectual religious debate with Jesus. So he invites Jesus over for a formal dinner at his home. Simon has all kinds of trick questions he's going to pose to Jesus to trap and embarrass Him. He is so excited, in fact, about getting into this religious alley fight that when Jesus finally shows up, Simon forgets all about the rudimentary courtesies of the day—the proper greeting and feet washing. Simon just says, "Sit right down. Sit right down," and starts asking his religious questions.

Midpoint through the conversation a woman with a shameful sexual past walks in unannounced and she notices that Jesus' feet have not been properly washed. In a very moving way, she washes His feet. Simon responds, "That settles it!" He was ready to throw out Jesus because one of the Pharisee's rules was that you could never touch someone with a shameful sexual past. And here's Jesus allowing this woman with a shameful sexual past to touch Him.

Jesus feels Simon's accusation coming and says, "Simon, maybe you have something important to say. But before you bring that up, can I ask you a question? You're a theological professor. Let me give you an exam. There's a creditor, and two people owe him money. One owes him just a little bit of money—$500. Another owes him $500,000. Out of a generous spirit the creditor decides to cancel both debts. Simon, here's the question: Which of the two debtors would be happiest?" He answers tentatively, "Well, I suppose the one who has been forgiven the greatest debt would be the happiest." Jesus says, "Very good, Simon. You got it right."

But then Jesus gets to the issue of Simon's hardheadedness. He points out that Simon was so anxious to get into an intellectual sparring match that he didn't even give a proper greeting or have a servant wash His feet. It's as if Jesus was saying to Simon, "There is not an ounce of honor, esteem, or worship in your heart for Me. That's the truth about you, Simon. While you were interested in an intellectual debate, a woman came in and tenderly washed My feet. I know her past and I have forgiven her. Her heart is so full of worship that she washed My feet with her tears. Simon, externally, you're doing good. You're hitting two thousand free throws in a row. You know lots of answers, and you have a sharp theological mind. She's got a past that is stained with sin, and if the truth is known, morally she couldn't hit three straight free throws if she tried. But in My eyes, because of the way the kingdom works, she just hit ten thousand straight. Her righteousness exceeds yours because she is righteous and worshipful to the core. It's a heart thing Simon. It's a heart thing."

4 What can cause you to sometimes be so hardheaded that doctrines and religious teachings end up being more important than following Jesus and loving others?

5 In this story a "sinful" woman ends up being declared righteous, and a "religious" man is forced to confront his own unrighteousness. How does this story act as a key to help us understand the true nature of righteousness?

In light of this story, how can our righteousness exceed that of the scribes and the Pharisees?

Read Snapshot "A Story of a Hard Heart"

A STORY OF A HARD HEART

In Mark 3 we find the story of a time Jesus was invited to speak in a Jewish synagogue—for all the wrong reasons. The scribes and Pharisees who invited Him didn't care about what He was going to say. Instead, they wanted to set Him up for a spiritual sting. Here's how it worked.

One of the laws of the Old Testament is, "Observe the Sabbath Day by keeping it holy. Six days you shall labor and do all your work, but the seventh day is a Sabbath to the LORD your God." Over time, the religious leaders had added many extensions to that law. You couldn't pick up a bucket on the Sabbath. You couldn't raise a certain size fork to your mouth. The list of Sabbath violations had grown longer and longer. Anything that vaguely resembled work was forbidden. Their goal was to catch Jesus "in the act" of breaking any of these laws and then to condemn Him for it.

Here's the set up. They invited Jesus to speak. After He agreed to come, they found a man with an unsightly, withered hand and brought him to hear Jesus, the Miracle Worker, speak. They were even conniving enough to give him a front row seat. He probably thought, "What a nice group of fellows." The truth is, their hearts were so hard that they didn't care about his needs. He was just a pawn in their plan to trap Jesus.

Jesus began to teach. Seeing the man's disfigurement, His heart was stirred with compassion. He stopped in the middle of His talk to care for this man in need. Every scribe and Pharisee in the room was salivating. They were ready to pounce on Him if He healed on the Sabbath. As Jesus assessed the situation, He became grieved and angered at the hardness of their hearts. It astounded Him that religious leaders could be so hard-hearted toward a person in need. And then Jesus said to them, "Look, we're in a religious facility existing for religious purposes. This place is filled with people with religious degrees. Yet it is all about the external—there's no love in the hearts of anybody in this room."

Everyone was breathless. This was a defining moment. What was Jesus going to do? He finally broke the silence, "There *is* love in this room. There's love in My heart for a person in need." And then He said to the man, "Be healed." The moment the healing took place, everybody else stood up and screamed, "Gotcha!" They emptied the place and went out to plot how they could destroy Jesus. Jesus was looking for those who would have soft hearts, but He only found a room full of religious people with hearts of stone.

6 As Jesus looked around that synagogue, He saw religious people with hearts of stone. What does Jesus see when He looks at the church today?

As Jesus looks upon you today, what are the areas in which He might see a hardness of heart?

7 What marks the life of a person who has a tender heart toward God?

What needs to happen for a hard heart to be broken and become tender toward God and others?

8 What role does worship play in developing a tender heart?

What would your life look like if it were marked by a heart of worship?

TENDER HEARTS

All of us have people in our lives who have tender hearts
toward God. They seem to be able to tune into God's heartbeat
and feel deeply about the things that matter to God. They are
encouraging and uplifting, because their hearts are soft toward
God. They may have impacted our lives in the past, and they
may be an inspiration and encouragement to us today.

Take time in the coming week to give the gift of gratitude to
those people in your life whose hearts are tender toward the
things of God. Thank them for the impact God has had on
your life through them. Encourage them to continue to be ten-
derhearted. Let them know their example is desperately needed, and that God is using them to have an impact on other
Christ followers. Be creative in expressing and delivering the
gift of gratitude.

Fixing Broken Relationships

Reflections from Session 2

1. Who is one person in your life who has a tender heart toward God? How has their example impacted your life?
2. What is one form or expression of worship that really brings you into the presence of God? How can you carve out time for worshiping God in this way?
3. Take a few moments as a group to choose a form of expressing worship. Spend a few moments during this meeting expressing your worship to God. Experiment. Take a "worship risk." God will be thrilled!

THE BIG PICTURE

I don't know if you've thought about it very much, but there is a kind of protocol that governs how people behave when they attend things like concerts, movies, plays, or church services. These rules are not written down anywhere, but we all have kind of a "sixth sense" or instinct about how people should conduct themselves in large public gatherings.

Arriving on time to a large public gathering is one of those rules we all would agree is important to follow. And after you have taken pains to arrive on time, have found your seat and settled in, you don't want the tardy bunch crawling all over you to get to their seats. That's breaking the rules!

Another rule is to be quiet and tune in to what's going on up front. Have you ever gone to a movie or play when someone talked or whispered throughout the whole show? That's really rude! It's so rude that we feel justified in glancing over our shoulder and giving them "the look."

There are many other unwritten rules for public gatherings, but there is one that seems to be the most important: *Don't leave until the meeting is over.* At the top of the rudeness list is walking out while a meeting is still in progress. In fact, getting up in a public place and walking out is often recognized as a form of protest. It makes a big statement to the people who stay. They wonder if it's something someone said, or if the person who walked out is fed up with this movie, this play, this musical number, this sermon. When you see someone stand up in the middle of a large public gathering, pack up their stuff, climb over people, and leave, you know something is probably very, very wrong.

A WIDE ANGLE VIEW

1 How do you react when someone breaks one of the unwritten rules of etiquette?

Read Snapshot "Etiquette in the First Century"

ETIQUETTE IN THE FIRST CENTURY

You can't imagine how stiff and formal the services were in Jesus' day. When you attended religious services in the first century, you showed up on time. You didn't even *think* about walking into a synagogue late. You didn't poke your neighbor, tell jokes during the service, wear your beeper, or answer your cellular phone. No, no, no! You didn't distract or harass anyone around you. And you can bet your life you didn't get up in front of everybody halfway through the sermon, climb over six people, and leave.

If the sermon had begun and you remembered the pot roast was set too high back home, you just considered it a burnt offering unto the Lord. If you were feeling deathly ill, like you might die any minute, you took comfort in knowing that your death would be duly acknowledged by the church leaders—*after the service.*

A BIBLICAL PORTRAIT

Read Matthew 5:21–26

2 Why do you think Jesus begins His teaching on anger and harsh words with a quotation of the Old Testament commandment, "Do not murder"?

SHARPENING THE FOCUS

Read Snapshot "Which Boat Are You In?"

WHICH BOAT ARE YOU IN?

Picture a dad who's going out fishing with his two sons. There's just one problem—his sons have had a falling out with each other. They're really angry with each other, but they both want to go fishing with their dad. So they're out in the boat, but even though they both think they can relate to their dad, every conversation is measured, every action carefully calculated. The father tries to engage each of the boys, but it is not easy. The odor of hostility in the boat is worse than the smell of the worms and the fish. By 9:00 A.M. they pack it up and head for the shore. They are not having fun. The family system is breaking down, and no one is having a good time.

Now imagine another boat where the dad is in the middle seat and both boys are getting along really great with each other. The atmosphere is charged with energy and humor. The conversations flow unedited. There's no walking on eggshells. Actions are spontaneous. The fishing is enjoyable enough, but what keeps the boat out on the lake until sunset is the quality of the family system. The richness of the community in all of its various dynamics brings a sweet aroma to everyone in the boat.

3 Jesus challenges us to look beyond overt sinful actions to the condition of our hearts. How can unresolved anger destroy our relationships with others?

How can unresolved anger toward others hurt our relationship with God?

4 How can harsh words damage our relationships with others? With God?

Did you ever wish you could take back some biting comments or harsh words?

5 Can you remember a time when you watched two people refuse to forgive each other? What were some of the consequences and results?

6 How is Christ dishonored when seekers watch us harbor bitterness and anger toward each other and refuse to seek healing in our relationships?

Read Snapshot "Critical Care"

CRITICAL CARE

Some time ago during an athletic event, I ruptured my Achilles tendon. I ruptured it on a Friday night. I went to the emergency room, and they said I was going to need surgery. I explained how busy my schedule was the next few days and that it would be helpful if surgery could wait until my schedule cleared. The doctor said, "Okay, just be careful."

The nature of the Achilles rupture allows for several days, even weeks, before you really have to have surgery. You're not going to hurt anything. Nothing is bleeding. Complications are not that severe if you wait for a little while.

Contrast this response to a doctor who discovers a ruptured appendix. When you rupture your appendix, you better get to a hospital *fast.* Forget any and all responsibilities and items on your schedule. If you don't get it taken care of right away, toxins will leak out of the appendix and spread throughout your body. It could be lights out . . . permanently. This situation calls for immediate and decisive action.

7 Why do you think Jesus gave people permission to walk out of worship if they needed to heal a relationship with a brother or sister?

8 Jesus used an illustration of settling accounts with an adversary before getting to court. Why does Jesus call us to seek reconciliation with such urgency?

9 How should we respond if the person we approach does not want to have the relationship restored?

10

When we choose to approach a brother or sister who has something against us, what are some specific things that will help us do this in a healing manner?

PUTTING YOURSELF IN THE PICTURE

SEEK HEALING

Take time before the next meeting to read the Lord's Prayer as recorded in Matthew 6:9–15. How do you feel when you read the words of Jesus recorded in verses 12, 14, and 15? Think about the following questions: How serious is Jesus about our need to extend forgiveness and seek healing in our relationships? What is one relationship you need to work at restoring and healing? Why is it important for you to start healing this relationship today? As you begin the process, let group members know how they can support you.

COMMIT TO MEMORIZING SCRIPTURE

Therefore, if you are offering your gift at the altar and there remember that your brother has something against you, leave your gift there in front of the altar. First go and be reconciled to your brother; then come and offer your gift (Matt. 5:23–24).

LOOKING, LUSTING, OR LOVING?

REFLECTIONS FROM SESSION 3

1. What steps have you taken to seek healing in a relationship since the last time your group met? What fruit have you seen from your efforts?
2. Is there a person you know with whom you need to begin the process of reconciliation but have been reluctant to contact? What can your group do to encourage you and help you start the healing process in this relationship?

THE BIG PICTURE

As we begin this session, I want to invite you to take a journey in your mind. Close your eyes and transport yourself mentally to your favorite vacation place. Pause for a moment and see the sights, hear the sounds, smell the aromas. Now, tell someone next to you where you are. Where is that favorite vacation place? Maybe you love the mountains with lush meadows, snow covered peaks, and cool, running streams. Perhaps you are a desert person who loves the dry air, hot sands, and the clear night sky unique to that region. Or maybe you love a beautiful beach setting with the sound of the crashing waves and the smell of a cool, salty sea breeze. Maybe one or two people pictured the big city. Some people actually like vacationing in the hustle and bustle of the city.

Now, transport yourself mentally to the home where you spent most of your time growing up. Go to the dinner table where you ate your meals as a family. What pictures come to the screen of your mind? Can you remember the seating order around the table? Can you picture your family members? Can you smell the food cooking on the stove?

Now, come back to the present. Don't you just marvel at the human ability to imagine? Try to imagine what your life would be like without imagination. You can't do it. You would blow a mental circuit trying to imagine away your imagination.

With the power of imagination, we can go places without moving a muscle. We can replay pleasant memories of the past without pushing a rewind button. We can project ourselves into future scenarios. We can paint pictures in our minds that the greatest artist could never reproduce. It stimulates creativity. It even helps us maintain a spirit of courage during times of difficulty, because we can imagine what life will be like when we get through those tough times. Imagination helps leaders develop a vision for the future of their organization. Imagination is a marvelous gift from the hand of our creative God.

A WIDE ANGLE VIEW

1 What are some of the benefits of having a good imagination?

How is imagination helpful in your line of work or in the course of your day?

A BIBLICAL PORTRAIT

Read Matthew 5:27–30

2 How can our imagination be used in ways that are not pleasing to God?

Why do you think Jesus makes a clear connection between the act of adultery and the practice of entertaining lustful thoughts?

3 How would you respond to a person who says, "There is nothing wrong with entertaining lustful thoughts as long as you don't act on them"?

SHARPENING THE FOCUS

Read Snapshot "A Broad Spectrum"

A BROAD SPECTRUM

Jesus makes a distinction when He talks about men and women looking at each other. He seems to indicate there is an appropriate and honorable way for men to look at women and for women to look at men. He is also clear that there is an inappropriate and dishonoring way. By saying, "Anyone who looks at a person lustfully has already committed adultery in his heart," He's saying that there's one way of looking that is healthy and then there's another way of looking—a destructive way. A broad range of attitudes exists between these two extremes.

If you look at the continuum below, you will see that the left side represents God's ideal. In the middle is the common thinking and behavior of society. On the far right side represents when lust runs wild, ruling the heart and mind.

God's ideal   Cultural norms   A lust-controlled heart

4 What are some words or statements that would describe each of these three places on the continuum?

- God's ideal

- Cultural norms

- A lust-controlled heart

Where would you place yourself on this continuum at this time in your life?

God's ideal   Cultural norms   A lust-controlled heart

Read Snapshot "Image Bearers"

IMAGE BEARERS

The Bible says that both men and women are image bearers of the Almighty God. There's a part to His character, His identity, His personality, His make-up that is resident within us. When a man looks upon a woman and when a woman looks upon a man, the ideal way of relating is to see a *multidimensional image-bearing person*. In other words, a man looks at a woman, realizes she has an intellectual side and wonders what this woman thinks about. He realizes she has an emotional side and wonders what she feels—what brings her joy and what causes sorrow in her life? He realizes she has a relational side and wonders what kind of family this woman came from and what her friendships are like. He sees the woman's spiritual dimension and wonders what she believes about God and faith. He notices the physical/sexual dimension and realizes there's a kind of sexual energy that comes from someone of the opposite sex.

The idea is that a man or a woman should look at a person of the opposite sex and want to enter into community in an honorable, God-fearing way with the whole person within biblical boundaries. God wants us to know others as whole people. When your imagination works in this ideal way of relating, you will have appropriate amounts of curiosity regarding each dimension of a person, and your relationships will be pure and God-honoring.

5

What can we do to discover the image-bearing, multi-dimensional aspects of the people we meet?

If we see each person we meet as a full image bearer of Almighty God, how does this impact the way we view those of the opposite sex?

Read Snapshot "Living in a Sin-stained World"

LIVING IN A SIN-STAINED WORLD

 The middle section of the continuum exists primarily because we live in a sin-stained world. We exist in a time when we are inundated with sexual images, tantalizing pictures, seductive models, magazines, and movies. This constant supply of images produces sexual energy in us that affects us in some pretty ill-defined and unpredictable ways.

We know what the ideal is, but we don't live in an ideal world. Because we have been saturated by the culture we live in, our view of the opposite sex can be tainted. When we meet someone we find attractive, we realize intuitively that this is a multidimensional creature—a full image bearer of God. But it isn't long before we tend to start focusing in on the physical/sexual dimension. Instead of only staying there for a little while and then quickly moving to the rest of what makes that person whole, we can get stuck on the physical side.

The Bible says we have control of our imagination to a large extent. We can commission our imaginations to move quickly off the physical/sexual dimension of the other person and start to ask questions about his or her ideas, feelings, family, and beliefs. But we can also commission our imaginations to run loose with the physical/sexual side of things and start a fascinating kind of motion picture in our heads that has a sexual orientation to it. We make the choice.

6

What are some of the primary sources of unhealthy sexual messages and images?

What can we do to reduce or cut off the supply line of these sources?

Read Snapshot "When Lust Runs Wild"

WHEN LUST RUNS WILD

Many people live their daily lives on the troubled side of the continuum where lust controls their heart. When someone on this end of the spectrum meets a person of the opposite sex, they tend to get riveted to the physical/sexual side of a person. If you struggle with this, you may have a very hard time commissioning your imagination to be interested in the other person. You just stay fired up about the physical/sexual side. It's the only thing you're really curious about. And if the person is especially attractive to you, later on you might think more about the physical/sexual side of that person, letting lustful thoughts become a preoccupation for days or weeks. What you'd really like is to be involved with them for the gratification of your sexual desires. I'm not trying to be harsh by stating things this clearly; I'm simply trying to describe the real-life patterns of many people.

On this end of the continuum, a man or woman's imagination works overtime to create exciting sexual escapades about the people they meet. But in fixating on that one dimension of a person, we begin to view them as existing for the primary purpose of satisfying sexual imaginations. He or she is no longer seen as someone who bears the image of God. This reductionary view of a human being breaks the heart of God.

7

What are some of the dangers or damaging results of a person living on this end of the continuum?

8

What practical steps can be taken in each area listed below:

- Cutting off the supply of whatever encourages lust in our lives

- Filling our minds with constructive images and information

- Building healthy and integrity-filled relationships that honor God

9 What can you do as a small group to help each other in each of these areas?

PUTTING YOURSELF IN THE PICTURE

CUTTING OFF THE SOURCE

Take time in the coming days to identify one or two primary sources of destructive and unhealthy images. What specific actions can you take to cut off the supply line of these harmful sources?

Source   Actions to cut off the supply

1.

2.

OUT WITH THE BAD AND IN WITH THE GOOD

The Bible is a primary source of good thoughts and images. Commit yourself to pouring the goodness of God's truth into your heart and mind by:

- reading at least a chapter from the Bible each day for the coming month
- memorizing Matthew 5:27–30 over the coming days

AN AUDIENCE OF ONE

REFLECTIONS FROM SESSION 4

1. What steps have you taken to cut off the supply of negative images to your heart and mind? How have you seen this help you develop a more God-honoring thought life?

2. What have you been doing to increase the intake of God-honoring images into your heart and mind? How have you seen this strengthen your ability to see others as multidimensional people who bear God's image?

THE BIG PICTURE

I don't know if the name Kevin McHale means anything to you. He's a retired NBA basketball player who played for the Boston Celtics. I once read an article he wrote in which he said some people are wringing their hands, wondering if the NBA can survive the retirement of so many great players. He wrote, "Don't worry about a thing. The league will survive just fine." He said, "Stars come and go. New stars are appearing on the scene every year."

Reading between the lines a bit, I think Kevin is being a bit sarcastic and maybe even a bit bitter. There was a time in his life when he enjoyed the applause of huge crowds in various auditoriums and arenas around the country. Now he's retired. He's not hearing applause anymore. He's not making the big shots to win the game and get the headlines. I think he's realizing that the applause of the masses is both fickle and fleeting. It never really satisfies, and it is never secure.

While watching a Chicago Bears game recently I mentioned that a particular running back made a move like Walter Payton. Half the room looked at me and said, "Walter who?" I thought, "You've got to be kidding. Walter Payton was a household name in the 1980s!" I guess that's the way fame works . . . here today and gone tomorrow.

A WIDE ANGLE VIEW

1 Who are some of the superstars that seem to have disappeared from the public spotlight over the past few years?

How might they feel when their time in the limelight is over?

A BIBLICAL PORTRAIT

Read Matthew 6:1–18

2 Jesus clearly calls His followers to live for an audience of One. All we do should be to please God and not the people around us. However, there is a human tendency, even among Christ followers, to do things to impress those around us.

What specific warnings are given to Christ followers in this passage?

Why do you think Jesus' warning is so strong?

SHARPENING THE FOCUS

Read Snapshot "A Serious Warning"

A SERIOUS WARNING

Orienting our lives around pleasing other people just sets us up for dissatisfaction and disillusion-ment. Jesus warns us to beware of living out our faith for other people. If we do everything for the sake of pleasing or impressing others, we will have no reward from our Father in heaven. Without doing any finger pointing and without seeking to shame us, Jesus simply says, "I want all of you to be attentive to the human tendency to please other people." And then He says, "Especially be careful not to spend all of your time trying to please other people when it comes to matters of your faith."

Jesus wants us to know that if we are not careful, it's possible to spend years attending Christian events, saying Christian things, doing Christian deeds, obeying Christian rules, and still wind up with only a little human applause when we come to the final day. He does not want us to end up with only a pat on the back from family and friends. He wants us to be certain of our standing in the kingdom of heaven.

In the final analysis, what's really important in life and eternity is pleasing God. Our lives should seek approval and affirmation from Him. When we work for the approval of people, we will often get it. But, in the process, we will miss the heavenly reward that lasts for eternity.

3 What are some of the areas in which Christ followers tend to perform for others rather than for God?

What is one area in which you sometimes do things to please people rather than God?

4 What are some of the consequences we might face if we live our lives for people rather than for God?

Read Snapshot "The Secrecy Test"

THE SECRECY TEST

Jesus asks His listeners three questions in the Secrecy Test:

Question one: How much money would you give kingdom causes if the only one who knew about it was God?

Question two: How often would you pray if no one else but God were keeping track?

Question three: How important would fasting be in your spiritual development if no one but God knew you were fasting?

If the offering plate was never passed, if you weren't concerned about your spouse complaining that you're cheap, if you weren't worried that your kids would grow up and see you not being a generous person, if all other people were out of the equation, how much money would you joyfully give to kingdom causes? If no one ever heard you pray or saw you bow your head or knew you took time to talk with God, how much time would you spend praying? If no one ever knew you were practicing the discipline of fasting, would you even bother doing it? If all of these religious actions were just between you and God, would you really spend a lot of time doing them?

5 Why are we so caught up with seeking approval?

What eternal rewards might we gain if we seek only to please God secretly?

Read Snapshot "An Essential Encounter"

AN ESSENTIAL ENCOUNTER

I want to present a hypothesis for your evaluation. You must decide if you agree with it:

Most of us approach Christianity with a people-pleasing bias. Until or unless we have a personal encounter with God Himself, we'll never break out of this people-pleasing pattern.

It's been my observation that people who genuinely orient their lives around pleasing God are those who have had unforgettable experiences or encounters with Him. People who are jumping through hoops and doing religious drills and going around looking for spiritual pats on the back are not bad people—they've just never really known God personally.

---

6 Describe a time when you had a personal encounter with God. How did that experience changed the way you live your life?

7 In light of the scriptural invitation, "Come near to God and He will come near to you," what are ways you can open yourselves to meaningful encounters with the living God?

PUTTING YOURSELF IN THE PICTURE

MOTIVE CHECK

At the heart of Jesus' teaching in this passage is the issue of our motives. What is the driving force in our lives? Do we seek to please God or people? Take time in the coming days to reflect honestly on the five areas listed below. Put an "X" on the line to mark where your life is today.

	100% for God	100% for people
Giving	├─────────────────────────────────┤
Praying	├─────────────────────────────────┤
Fasting	├─────────────────────────────────┤
Serving	├─────────────────────────────────┤
Worship	├─────────────────────────────────┤

What must change in your heart to move each mark toward being 100 percent for God?

MAKING SPACE FOR GOD

If we are going to encounter God in the course of our day, we need to learn how to make space in our hectic schedules to slow down and be still. A quiet place where we can pray, journal, read the Bible, listen, and meet God is essential. Consider the three challenges below as you look at your calendar and plan for the coming month:

- Schedule thirty minutes a day for time alone with God.
- Schedule a two-hour period once a week for prayer and reflection.
- Block out a twenty-four hour period in the next month for a personal retreat where you spend an entire day alone with God. If you commit to this, meet with a pastor or Christian you respect to discuss ideas for how you can use this time to focus your heart on God.

WHY WORRY?

REFLECTIONS FROM SESSION 5

1. How have you been seeking to create space in your life to encounter God? How have you sensed God meeting you in this time and speaking to you?
2. If you have had meaningful encounters with God over the past few weeks, how have these experiences caused you to want to live your life for an audience of One?

THE BIG PICTURE

Some time ago I had dinner with a guy who owns a bungee-jumping company. In the course of our discussion, he shared something that did not surprise me. He told me that "pretty much everyone is afraid." He said, "You know, Bill, when they're up on the platform that gives way to the water below and they're all strapped in and ready to jump, I can see it in their eyes." He continued, "Some people mask their fear with acts of bravado, but it's still there. They want to experience the thrill of a long free fall, but there's another side of them that says 'I'm scared to take the plunge.'"

As Jesus preached the Sermon on the Mount, He addressed the tough topic of changing focus from earthly treasures to heavenly ones. He told the people that they needed to relax their grip on the acquisition and enjoyment of earthly things and to firm up their grip on treasures that would last forever. I think that when Jesus started talking this way, some people got a little scared.

Fear is a powerful emotion. Sometimes it short-circuits those decisions of faith that need to be made as you walk with God. Deciding to take the dive into full devotion and complete commitment to God can lead to fear and anxiety.

In this section of the Sermon on the Mount, Jesus is giving people like us a message of encouragement to dive into full devotion to God. You will hear Him say, "Let's suppose you take the dive. Let's suppose you stand on that bungee-jumping platform of faith and say, 'I think I trust the Father enough to dive into full devotion. I'm going to clear up my eyesight and focus on that which is eternal. I'm going to choose the right Master, follow Him, and do His bidding—whatever it costs. I'm taking that dive.'" Jesus says, "Go ahead and jump. And while you're free falling, I've got some words of comfort for you. I've got some "don't-worry-about-it" kinds of truths I want to give you so that you'll be able to enjoy the free fall and not be fearful about it."

A WIDE ANGLE VIEW

1 Describe those times when you experience fear or anxiety in your life.

A BIBLICAL PORTRAIT

Read Matthew 6:25–34

2 According to the words of Jesus in this section of the Sermon on the Mount, why can we live a worry-free life?

How have you seen faith in God remove or reduce worry in your life?

SHARPENING THE FOCUS

Read Snapshot "You Are More Than Just a Body"

YOU ARE MORE THAN JUST A BODY

The first reason for not worrying once we take the dive comes right out of Matthew 6:25, "Therefore I tell you, do not worry about your life, what you will eat or drink; or about your body, what you will wear." And here's the phrase I want to focus on: "Is not life more important than food, and the body more important than clothes?" Here's Jesus' argument—reason number one—to take the plunge. You shouldn't worry so much about your future because human beings are more than bodies.

Listen closely to His rationale. If we were just bodies, if we were only here for seventy years and then gone forever, then it would make complete sense to pay ultimate attention to our bodies. But we are far more than just bodies. In fact, it's what's inside these physical bodies that really matters in the scope of eternity. Jesus is not discounting the physical body, but He does place the importance on what's inside. God gave you a heart and a soul and a mind. He's given you a personality and a conscience and feelings and aspirations and affections. You are so much more than just a body! He says, "My Father breathed His breath inside your body. My Father put a soul inside your body. My Father has sought to relate to the heart He put inside your body."

3

What drives us to spend so much time worrying about our physical well-being?

If you spend more time caring for your outer appearance than your inner person, what can you do to grow more balanced in this area of life? How would that look?

4

God also promises to care for His creation. How does your awareness of this commitment make you feel about His promise to provide for you?

Read Snapshot "Worry Does Not Change Things"

WORRY DOES NOT CHANGE THINGS

Another reason Jesus encourages people to stop worrying is found in verse 27: "Who of you by worrying can add a single hour to his life?" Jesus tells us not to worry so much after taking the plunge because worry doesn't produce anything constructive. In fact, worry can do enormous physiological and psychological damage to your life. I think Jesus is poking a little fun here to lighten things up a bit. He's talking to people who worry a lot and inviting them to give a little feedback. It's like He's saying, "When you commit yourself to the production of ferocious anxiety and worry, does it work? Does it produce good things? Can you manipulate events? Can you change stuff if you really worry hard?" He's asking, "If you're short and you'd like to be taller, does worry produce greater height? Does it bump you up an inch or two? If you're worrying about dying prematurely, will a ferocious commitment to fretting over that possibility add a few bonus years to your life? Jesus' answer is, "I think not." His message is the same today as it was two thousand years ago: Stop worrying—it doesn't produce anything constructive.

5

What are some of the hurtful and negative results of worry and anxiety?

- Emotionally

- Physically

- Relationally

- Spiritually

Read Snapshot "Humans Last Longer Than Flowers"

HUMANS LAST LONGER THAN FLOWERS

Yet another reason Jesus says to go ahead and take the plunge into full devotion to the Father without worry comes out of verses 28–30: "And why do you worry about clothes? See how the lilies of the field grow. They do not labor or spin. Yet I tell you that not even Solomon in all his splendor was dressed like one of these. If that is how God clothes the grass of the field, which is here today and tomorrow is thrown into the fire, will he not much more clothe you, O you of little faith?" Why should we worry less when our lives are in the hand's of God? Because humans last longer than flowers. Listen to Jesus' logic here. He is saying, "Some of you think that if you follow Me fully you'll be the laughingstock of your peers because you won't even have the resources to appropriately clothe yourself. But don't worry about your clothes. My Father has that covered. Here's the proof. Look at the lily. It's stunning. It's breathtaking. It's beautiful. The lily doesn't worry or fret about its fashion design. It doesn't beg or barter to gain its beauty. The lily just sort of looks up and says, 'Dress me, God.' And not only does God dress the lily, but He gives it clothing more beautiful than Solomon, the smartest, wealthiest, most fashion-conscious human being in history."

---

6 Jesus says, "Do not worry about what you will wear." Describe worry-free shopping and anxiety-free dressing.

Why is it so difficult to stop worrying about these things?

7 If Jesus calls us to trust in our heavenly Father to meet our needs, how do we determine what we "need" and what we really "want?" Give specific examples.

8 How have you seen God meet your needs over the past year?

What is one serious need you have in your life right now? Is it hard trusting God to meet that need? If so, why?

Read Snapshot "God Keeps His Promises"

GOD KEEPS HIS PROMISES

The final reason Jesus says we can take the dive in commitment to God and not worry so much about the consequences comes out of Matthew 6:33: "But seek first his kingdom and his righteousness, and all these things will be given to you as well." We can take the dive and not worry, because God will fulfill His promise. What is His promise? That if you put Him, His purposes, and His kingdom first, you will be first on *His* agenda. All the things mentioned in this text will be given to you. What are some of those things? Jesus is talking about the necessities of life, not necessarily all the luxuries of life. He promises us daily bread, appropriate clothing, acceptable shelter, and other basic provisions of life. God promises to come through for those of us who take the dive into full devotion and seek first His kingdom.

9

What will it mean for you to "Seek first the kingdom of God" in your life in the coming week?

10

What is one area of your life in which you are "holding out" and having trouble giving it to God?

Discuss ways the group can encourage each other as you seek to surrender these areas of your lives to God?

PUTTING YOURSELF IN THE PICTURE

THANK YOU FOR MEETING MY NEEDS

Take time in the coming days to thank God for meeting your needs. It is so easy to focus on the things we don't have or the things we want. Sometimes we need to turn our focus back on how much God has given us and how much He does for us each day. Use the guideline below to direct you in thanking

God for meeting your needs. You may want to pray silently, with a group, or write your prayer of thanksgiving in a journal.

Take time to thank God for:

- providing for your material needs
- giving you people who love and care for you
- sending His only Son to die so that you could live forever
- establishing His church as a place you can grow, worship, serve, and be equipped to reach out to seekers with God's love
- providing this group as a place to gain support and prayer

BALANCING THE INNER AND OUTER LIFE

If you spend more time each day caring for your outward appearance than you do developing your life as a follower of Christ, what can you do to shift more of the focus onto developing your inner life of faith? If you spend excessive time on your outward appearance, commit some of this time to developing your relationship with Jesus. Set specific goals for the time you want to spend in prayer, journaling, meditation, and study of the Bible, and communicate this to a member of your small group. Have them pray for you and keep you accountable.

LEADER'S NOTES

Leading a Bible discussion—especially for the first time—can make you feel both nervous and excited. If you are nervous, realize that you are in good company. Many biblical leaders, such as Moses, Joshua, and the apostle Paul, felt nervous and inadequate to lead others (see, for example, 1 Corinthians 2:3). Yet God's grace was sufficient for them, just as it will be for you.

Some excitement is also natural. Your leadership is a gift to the others in the group. Keep in mind, however, that other group members also share responsibility for the group. Your role is simply to stimulate discussion by asking questions and encouraging people to respond. The suggestions listed below can help you to be an effective leader.

PREPARING TO LEAD

1. Ask God to help you understand and apply the passage to your own life. Unless that happens, you will not be prepared to lead others.
2. Carefully work through each question in the study guide. Meditate and reflect on the passage as you formulate your answers.
3. Familiarize yourself with the leader's notes for each session. These will help you understand the purpose of the session and will provide valuable information about the questions in the session.
4. Pray for the various members of the group. Ask God to use these sessions to make you better disciples of Jesus Christ.
5. Before the first session, make sure each person has a study guide. Encourage them to prepare beforehand for each session.

LEADING THE SESSION

1. Begin the session on time. If people realize that the session begins on schedule, they will work harder to arrive on time.
2. At the beginning of your first time together, explain that these sessions are designed to be discussions, not lectures. Encourage everyone to participate, but realize some may be hesitant to speak during the first few sessions.

3. Don't be afraid of silence. People in the group may need time to think before responding.

4. Avoid answering your own questions. If necessary, rephrase a question until it is clearly understood. Even an eager group will quickly become passive and silent if they think the leader will do most of the talking.

5. Encourage more than one answer to each question. Ask, "What do the rest of you think?" or "Anyone else?" until several people have had a chance to respond.

6. Try to be affirming whenever possible. Let people know you appreciate their insights into the passage.

7. Never reject an answer. If it is clearly wrong, ask, "Which verse led you to that conclusion?" Or let the group handle the problem by asking them what they think about the question.

8. Avoid going off on tangents. If people wander off course, gently bring them back to the passage being considered.

9. Conclude your time together with conversational prayer. Ask God to help you apply those things that you learned in the session.

10. End on time. This will be easier if you control the pace of the discussion by not spending too much time on some questions or too little on others.

We encourage all small group leaders to use *Leading Life-Changing Small Groups* (Zondervan) by Bill Donahue while leading their group. Developed and used by Willow Creek Community Church, this guide is an excellent resource for training and equipping followers of Christ to effectively lead small groups. It includes valuable information on how to utilize fun and creative relationship-building exercises for your group; how to plan your meeting; how to share the leadership load by identifying, developing, and working with an "apprentice leader"; and how to find creative ways to do group prayer. In addition, the book includes material and tips on handling potential conflicts and difficult personalities, forming group covenants, inviting new members, improving listening skills, studying the Bible, and much more. Using *Leading Life-Changing Small Groups* will help you create a group that members love to be a part of.

Now let's discuss the different elements of this small group study guide and how to use them for the session portion of your group meeting.

THE BIG PICTURE

Each session will begin with a short story or overview of the lesson theme. This is called "The Big Picture" because it introduces the central theme of the session. You will need to read this section as a group or have group members read it on their own before discussion begins. Here are three ways you can approach this section of the small group session:

- As the group leader, read this section out loud for the whole group and then move into the questions in the next section, "A Wide Angle View." (You might read the first week, but then use the other two options below to encourage group involvement.)
- Ask a group member to volunteer to read this section for the group. This allows another group member to participate. It is best to ask someone in advance to give them time to read over the section before reading it to the group. It is also good to ask someone to volunteer, and not to assign this task. Some people do not feel comfortable reading in front of a group. After a group member has read this section out loud, move into the discussion questions.
- Allow time at the beginning of the session for each person to read this section silently. If you do this, be sure to allow enough time for everyone to finish reading so they can think about what they've read and be ready for meaningful discussion.

A WIDE ANGLE VIEW

This section includes one or more questions that move the group into a general discussion of the session topic. These questions are designed to help group members begin discussing the topic in an open and honest manner. Once the topic of the lesson has been established, move on to the Bible passage for the session.

A BIBLICAL PORTRAIT

This portion of the session includes a Scripture reading and one or more questions that help group members see how the theme of the session is rooted and based in biblical teaching. The Scripture reading can be handled just like "The Big Picture" section: You can read it for the group, have a group member read it, or allow time for silent reading. Make sure everyone has a Bible or that you have Bibles available for those who need them. Once you have read the passage, ask the question(s) in this section so that group members can dig into the truth of the Bible.

SHARPENING THE FOCUS

The majority of the discussion questions for the session are in this section. These questions are practical and help group members apply biblical teaching to their daily lives.

SNAPSHOTS

The "Snapshots" in each session help prepare group members for discussion. These anecdotes give additional insight to the topic being discussed. Each "Snapshot" should be read at a designated point in the session. This is clearly marked in the session as well as in the leader's notes. Again, follow the same format as you do with "The Big Picture" section and the "Biblical Portrait" section: Either you read the anecdote, have a group member volunteer to read, or provide time for silent reading. However you approach this section, you will find these anecdotes very helpful in triggering lively dialogue and moving discussion in a meaningful direction.

PUTTING YOURSELF IN THE PICTURE

Here's where you roll up your sleeves and put the truth into action. This portion is very practical and action-oriented. At the end of each session there will be suggestions for one or two ways group members can put what they've just learned into practice. Review the action goals at the end of each session and challenge group members to work on one or more of them in the coming week.

You will find follow-up questions for the "Putting Yourself in the Picture" section at the beginning of the next week's session. Starting with the second week, there will be time set aside at the beginning of the session to look back and talk about how you have tried to apply God's Word in your life since your last time together.

PRAYER

You will want to open and close your small group with a time of prayer. Occasionally, there will be specific direction within a session for how you can do this. Most of the time, however, you will need to decide the best place to stop and pray. You may want to pray or have a group member volunteer to begin the lesson with a prayer. Or you might want to read "The Big Picture" and discuss the "Wide Angle View" questions before opening in prayer. In some cases, it might be best to open in prayer after you have read the Bible passage. You need to decide where you feel an opening prayer best fits for your group.

When opening in prayer, think in terms of the session theme and pray for group members (including yourself) to be responsive to the truth of Scripture and the working of the Holy Spirit. If you have seekers in your group (people investigating Christianity but not yet believers) be sensitive to your expectations for group prayer. Seekers may not yet be ready to take part in group prayer.

Be sure to close your group with a time of prayer as well. One option is for you to pray for the entire group. Or you might allow time for group members to offer audible prayers that others can agree with in their hearts. Another approach would be to allow a time of silence for one-on-one prayers with God and then to close this time with a simple "Amen."

HANGING ON FOR HEAVEN

MATTHEW 5:10–12

INTRODUCTION

This session focuses on gaining certainty about where we will spend eternity and how this certainty affects the way we live our lives. Jesus is crystal clear about two things in this section of the Sermon on the Mount. First, followers of Christ will face sufferings and persecution. Second, whatever we face, our reward in heaven is worth it!

Things have not changed all that much in the past two thousand years when it comes to suffering for Christ. Christians, especially in some parts of the world, still face persecution, and the hope of heaven's rewards still helps us hang on. Pray for yourself and your group members to get a tighter grasp on the joys and rewards of heaven and a deeper commitment to stand strong for Christ no matter what the cost.

THE BIG PICTURE

Take time to read this introduction with the group. There are suggestions for how this can be done in the beginning of this leader's section.

A WIDE ANGLE VIEW

Question One Heaven is sometimes referred to symbolically in Scripture as a city. That doesn't mean a city like Chicago with signs and curbs and gutters. The image of a city depicts a community. Heaven is a community of people where there are relationships with uninterrupted love and sensitivity. Perfect community.

You might have heard about mansions in heaven. These are also symbolic. The idea is that each person will be safe and secure. We will not be exposed to anything dangerous or harmful. There will be protection for every single individual. Freedom from fear. Freedom from anxiety and worry. God will protect us and keep us secure.

The Bible also talks about white robes. This image assures us that we will be able to walk around without shame. Without any remorse. Without any lingering sense of defeat due to sin or foul-ups.

When we hear of streets of gold it means heaven will be an exhilarating existence. There will be growth and change and wonder and beauty and challenge. It will be exhilarating.

The Bible also talks about a throne. The idea is not so much that thrones are great, but the One who sits on the throne rules forever. We'll be with God for eternity. I don't know if there is someone in your life that you love to be with. Maybe it's a relative that you only see a couple of times a year, or a close friend in a distant city. Whoever it is, multiply your longing to be with them by the largest number you know, and you'll get just a little sense of what the Bible means when it says you'll spend an adventurous eternity with the God of the universe.

A BIBLICAL PORTRAIT

Read Matthew 5:10–12

Question Three One of the central themes of Scripture is found in this passage. Jesus says, "Find out what it takes to get to heaven and get on board." Jesus once asked a group of very intelligent people, "Why would you gain this world if it means you have to give up heaven in the next?" That doesn't even make good common sense. You are going to be in the afterlife a whole lot longer than you are going to be in this life. You're going to be in that life forever. So whatever you have to go through in this life to wind up in the right place in the next life, get it done.

In the beginning of the greatest sermon in history, the Sermon on the Mount, Jesus describes what true Christianity is and invites people to accept it. He says, "Spiritual foul-ups are welcome." You know, "Blessed are the poor in spirit. They can have the kingdom of heaven." He continues by saying that those who are sorrowing are welcome. Gentle types are welcome, too. Those hungering to be made right with God, will be. Mercy givers will be rewarded. The pure in heart, the peacemakers will also be rewarded. Jesus has been describing His kingdom. He's been inviting people into it passionately and sincerely.

At this point in the sermon, Jesus takes a kind of turn and says, "Blessed are you who are going to pay a price for believing in Me and for coming into My kingdom. For great is your reward in heaven." And all of a sudden a collective gulp could be heard throughout the crowd. What is this about a price? How high is the price? What will the toll be?

Summarizing Jesus' words, I would say that heaven will make whatever price you had to pay to follow Jesus on earth worth it. Jesus does not promise an easy road for His followers. Quite the opposite. He guarantees a tough one. But He says, "It will be worth it in spades . . . in heaven."

There was a gulp in that crowd on the hillside a couple of thousand years ago. And maybe there's a lump in your throat today. Maybe you're saying, "Well, we don't hear much about price paying these days. The days of Christians being fed to lions are over, aren't they? The days of persecution are over, aren't they?" Well no, not entirely. What Jesus was saying to that crowd, He would just as easily say if He were speaking to you today. He would say, "My followers are going to pay a price for believing in Me and for living for Me. They always have, and they always will."

SHARPENING THE FOCUS

Question Four Maybe I can give you a quick overview of why Christ followers will pay a price for being true to Him. The first reason is that the value system of Jesus and the value system of contemporary society are always in conflict with each other. There are collisions between those people who approach life from a Christian perspective and those who don't. We see these fender benders happen in society all the time.

One obvious example is the terrible problem of irresponsible sexual expression that is causing unwanted pregnancies by the tens of thousands in our society and sexually transmitted diseases in the tens of millions. It is a major problem. This problem of careless sexuality is being adressed all over the land. The culture says it is a condom problem with a condom solution. But Christ followers say it's a character problem, a moral problem with spiritual roots. And the solution isn't for sale in vending machines on service station rest room walls. The Christian says, "Sin distorts our entire understanding of life, including our understanding of sexuality and how to express it. And the only way to neutralize and overcome sin is through salvation in Christ." When a Christian goes on public record with a statement like that, he or she is going to feel some heat. It's a head-on collision between the value system of the world and the value system of Christ. Suddenly, the battle lines are drawn and everybody sees the true color of each person's uniform.

I remember being in a university classroom on a very liberal campus some time ago. I was asked about my views on homosexuality and abortion. I took a deep breath and waved a quick good-bye to the warm rapport that I worked so hard to establish. I then explained as lovingly, as graciously, as nonjudgmentally, but as truthfully as I knew how, what the Bible says about those issues. I concluded by saying that my personal views are in line with the scriptural views on those matters. And in some regions of that classroom, the temperature dropped fifteen degrees. Suddenly, they looked at me differently. By merely articulating the basic position of Christ on those issues, I was immediately perceived as someone with a value system in direct opposition to the prevailing system of the world. The smiles faded and the frowns and looks of hostility formed, and it was tough getting through the rest of the class.

If you're true to your Christian convictions and you verbalize them, you are going to feel some heat. In case you haven't figured it out yet, it's not politically correct to be a dedicated Christ follower these days. Your numbers slide in many circles. Your overnight Nielsen ratings take a beating when you stand for basic Christian beliefs and values that our culture finds so narrow.

I was having a very stimulating and quite intellectually oriented discussion with a guy once. All was going well. We were relating in a highly charged way intellectually. And then he found out I was a Christian. He turned to me and said, "The kind that actually believes in God? The Bible? Heaven and hell?" I said, "Yeah." And then came the look. He rolled his eyes and I felt as if he thought, "You pathetic person. Your naiveté is only eclipsed by your ignorance." The temperature in that room also dropped substantially. Let's face it, attitudes toward Christ's followers have not changed much in two thousand years.

Read Snapshot "Moral Irritations" before Question 5

Question Five A fully devoted follower of Christ can really be an irritation in the marketplace. He's not trying to rub anybody's face in anything. She's not trying to expose or embarrass anybody. He's not making himself a nuisance or a pain in the name of Christ. She's just going about her work in a God-honoring way. But because he or she plays it straight with the expense account and doesn't permanently borrow company supplies, some people feel threatened. Because he doesn't plunder the company perk chest, puts in a full day's work for a full day's pay, and refuses to play politics, some other employees can become resentful. Before you know it, he's a curve buster. She's a pain. He's a moral irritation to the rest of the work force. Pretty soon someone thinks or actually comes out and says, "Would you get off your high horse? Stop thinking that you're better than the rest of us. All you Christians are alike. You're a bunch of self-righteous brownnosers who are trying to make the rest of us look bad. Knock it off."

What's really going on here? Is the Christian grandstanding? Hopefully not. But whenever someone in our circle messes up the grading curve, whether it's the academic grading curve or the moral grading curve, the curve buster is going to be ostracized. And if you've ever felt frozen out because you were trying to lead a God-honoring life, Jesus says, "I've got a kind word for you. Stand firm and smile, knowing that your reward will be great in heaven."

Along these lines, I remember talking to a married woman who had a pretty good marriage until she became a Christian and began to grow. This woman didn't lose any love for her husband, she just sort of fell out of love with rooms full of inebriated people. It wasn't fun for her anymore. So she diplomatically tried to put fewer parties on her and her husband's calendar. Also, her husband used to love to have his wife watch pornographic videos with him at night. She never really liked them much, but she went along with it until after her conversion. She then learned how destructive pornography can be to a person's sexuality. So she started to opt out of those late-night video viewings too. She didn't shame or slam dunk her husband. She just quietly opted out. The combination of fewer parties and fewer video sessions eventually led to the fateful night when her husband blew his stack and told her that he had had it up to here with all of her preaching and pressure and self-righteous behavior. And if she didn't stop her Pollyanna parading around, he was going to hit the road. Do you see what happened there? In reality, she wasn't preaching or pressuring or parading around. But her transformed life—her new values, attitudes, and behaviors—were creating an enormous moral irritation in the life of her husband, who all of a sudden had his moral backside exposed and didn't like the feeling. Nobody does. So what did he do? He did what Jesus predicted people would do. Using Jesus' words now, "He insulted, persecuted and falsely said all kinds of evil against you because of me."

Another reason Christ followers are likely to take some hits in this world is because someday many, if not most, of us are probably going to be lumped in with someone's worst experience with a religious person or group.

Some time ago I was at the Harvard Business School. They did a case study on Willow Creek Community Church some years ago, and it is studied each semester by the second-year graduate students. They study twenty-nine cases. Most of them are of multinational corporations. And right in the middle of it is this case on Willow Creek Community Church in South Barrington, Illinois. So they bring me out, and I listen to the cases that are being discussed in the class. At the end of the class I talk a little bit and take questions from the students. Most of the time, these are very friendly exchanges. But this one week, there was a guy who could not resist lumping me in with some prominent televangelists who had gotten caught in sexual and financial improprieties, and also with David Koresh, the cult leader from Waco, Texas, of all people. I'm sitting right in the classroom while he's taking these shots and lumping me in with those guys. Let me tell you, if you have never been in that kind of situation, it is a very uncomfortable feeling to be unfairly lumped in with people like that. But it's inevitable.

We will all get stereotyped and lumped in together sometimes. If it hasn't happened to you yet, it's going to. What do you do? What do you do when you get unfairly lumped in with some fringe elements of Christianity and it hurts you? Jesus says two things. First, stand firm. Live honorably. Live lovingly. Keep taking relational risks. And second, smile on the inside knowing that heaven will make it all worthwhile. We need to be forever people. But whatever you do, don't cave in. Don't shrink back.

Read Snapshot "Stand Firm and Smile" before Question 6

Question Six Allow time for group members to discuss ways they have discovered to stand strong in their faith even when they face the pain of persecution. Also, you may want to talk about the difference between putting a fake grin on your face and pretending everything is fine, and smiling on the inside even when situations are painful.

Jesus is not telling us to deny the struggles of living for Him. He certainly is not telling us to act as though things are fine and to act as if we don't need anyone else's help. Smiling on the inside is about realizing that, while today might be tough, our certainty of eternity with Jesus will make it all worthwhile.

Read Snapshot "What If?" before Question 7

Question Seven Jesus was not just blowing smoke when He talked about persecution. He knew what was going to unfold in just a couple of decades. The single most intense time of persecution of Christians in the history of the world was just around the corner. People who were right there on the hillside that day were going suffer because of their faith in ways they couldn't imagine.

People were going to be tortured, sawed in half, and burned to death for admitting to be Christ followers. So here's Jesus, knowing what's coming, giving His words of encouragement, "Blessed are you who stand firm. When you take ridicule, when you take beatings and endure torture . . . Blessed are you who stand firm." He wanted them to remember to smile on the inside because their reward would be great in heaven.

And so from the pages of church history we read of families—moms and dads and circles of kids—standing in the Colloseum holding hands as the lions are about ready to be released out of their cages. There they stand, singing worship songs, moments away from the time when they will be tortured and killed for believing in and following Christ. And they're singing worship songs because they said, "Great will be our reward in heaven. The Master said so."

PUTTING YOURSELF IN THE PICTURE

Let the group members know you will be providing time at the beginning of the next session for them to discuss how they have put their faith into action. Let them tell about how they have acted on one of the two options listed for this section. However, don't limit their interaction to these two options. They may have put themselves into the picture in some other way. Allow for honest and open communication.

Also, be clear that there will not be any kind of a "test" or forced reporting. All you are going to do is allow time for people to volunteer to talk about how they have applied what they learned in your last session. Some group members will feel pressured if they think you are going to make everyone report on how they acted on these action goals. You don't want anyone to skip the next session because they are afraid of having to say they did not follow up on what they learned from the prior session. The key is to provide a place for honest communication without creating pressure or fear of embarrassment.

Every session from this point on will open with a look back at the "Putting Yourself in the Picture" section of the previous session.

DEVELOPING A HEART OF FAITH

MATTHEW 5:17—20

INTRODUCTION

In this session Jesus drops a bombshell on all those who trust in their own righteousness to make them acceptable before the Father. He says, "Unless your righteousness (your morality, ethics, character, and goodness) surpasses that of the Pharisees and the teachers of the law, you will certainly not enter the kingdom of heaven." That was just like throwing a hand grenade into the crowd. You see, the scribes and Pharisees were the world record holders of righteousness. They had quit their jobs to do righteousness full time. They were addicted to righteousness. Not only did they obey the Scriptures, they made up several hundred additional laws to protect their behavior so they would never even risk getting outside the fence of righteousness. If anyone could make 2,036 spiritual free throws in a row, it was the scribes and the Pharisees. Then Jesus said to the crowd of people listening to Him, "Unless your righteousness surpasses theirs, you will certainly not enter the kingdom of heaven." There's the bomb.

These words are just as explosive today as they were 2,000 years ago. Jesus still wants us to know that the standard He requires is absolutely out of our reach. On our own, we are too hardheaded, hard-hearted, and sinful. However, He has made a way for us to be more righteous than the most law-abiding Pharisee.

THE BIG PICTURE

Take time to read this introduction with the group. There are suggestions for how this section of the study can be used in the beginning of the leader's section.

A WIDE ANGLE VIEW

Question One What could Jesus possibly mean when He tells us that we will never enter heaven unless our righteousness is greater than that of the spiritual marathon runners of

His day? How big a duffle bag would it take to hold all those certificates and trophies of personal righteousness?

In the fifth chapter of Matthew Jesus asks some tough questions. He says, "You're all pretty proud of the fact that you've never committed cold-blooded murder. Probably none of you in this crowd has stabbed anybody to death. But between you and Me, do you hate anybody? Is there anybody you just don't like? Might you even take pleasure if hard times came their way? Just wondering." Then He says, "Most of you have probably never committed adultery. But between you and Me, do you sometimes think about exciting sexual encounters with people other than your spouse? Or if you're single, do you let lust run wild in your heart and mind? Have you ever reduced a full image bearer of God to a sex object for your own gratification? Just wondering." Then He deals with truthful speech and says, "Most of you would probably tell the whole truth and nothing but the truth in a court of law. But, do you always tell the truth and keep your word in the course of your daily life? Or do you say the check is in the mail when you know it's not? Do you cut corners and say untruthful things? Just wondering."

In the Sermon on the Mount Jesus raises the standard of righteousness and calls people to a standard far beyond the simple letter of the Law. Far beyond the reach of even the most devoted scribe or Pharisee.

A Biblical Portrait

Read Matthew 5:17–20

Question Three Jesus is saying, "No longer are righteousness meters going to be strapped on the hands and feet and eyes and ears and tongues of people in order to find out if there is external compliance with kingdom standards of righteousness. No! It's a new day. From now on, righteousness meters are going to be strapped *on the hearts of people*. And those righteousness meters are going to monitor the hidden condition and motivations of the heart."

Jesus is saying, "In My kingdom, external compliance to kingdom commandments isn't enough. Your heavenly Father is not going to be satisfied with merely outside compliance. I'm looking for people whose spirituality emanates the radically transformed heart of a grace-invaded core. Skin-deep spirituality and cosmetic conformity to kingdom standards is not acceptable. I'm asking people to be righteous to the core—ten thousand consecutive free throws."

This theme is a hallmark theme in Jesus' teaching ministry. Almost every time Jesus turns around, almost everywhere He goes, someone bumps up against Him and wants to have a skin-deep conversation about some spiritual minutiae. They want to spar with Him concerning kingdom cosmetics. You know, Sabbath day restrictions, dietary customs, tithing and temple protocol, and nuances of Old Testament interpretation. Over and over we see Jesus gently turning the focus of the conversation from a skin-deep level to a probing, heart-exposing level. Jesus wants to get at what's really going on in their hearts.

Here's thekey to understanding Jesus' message: Once he touches and transforms our hearts, we inherit His heart and become righteous. We can't meet His high standard in our own righteousness, but we can inherit His righteousness. Once we do, we can live with confidence because Jesus shoots ten thousand consecutive free throws every time He steps up to the line!

SHARPENING THE FOCUS

Read Snapshot "A Story of a Hardhead" before Question 4

Question Five Jesus went after Simon, the theological professor, because he had a head full of knowledge, but he didn't have a heart of worship. His head was as hard as a rock, and his attitude would not allow him to worship Jesus. He had lots of religion but no relationship with the Savior. But Simon is not alone. There are quite a few present-day Simons out there who need someone to break through the granite walls that block out the love of God. You might be one of them.

Read Snapshot "A Story of a Hard Heart" before Question 6

Question Six Jesus went after the scribes and Pharisees because they didn't have a heart of love. The essence of Christianity is when people have hearts that are worshipful toward God because they've received and are grateful for what Christ did for them on the cross. And hearts full of worship toward God result in hearts full of love toward people.

If Jesus could visit your small group for an hour, He wouldn't go around and check your spiritual merit badges. They wouldn't interest Him much. He would want to know if your heart is full of worship. Are you undone once in awhile because of what He did for you on the cross? He would want to know if your heart is full of worship and if you have a passion for loving people. Is that a fair description of your heart? If it is, then your righteousness exceeds that of the scribes and the Pharisees. If not, no outward actions will prove you righteous in God's sight.

Questions Seven & Eight If your heart feels lifeless, do you know what the problem might be? You might be dead. If you are, that's serious. The good news is, you don't have to remain so, because God's Word says in Ephesians 2:4–5, "But because of his great love for us, God, who is rich in mercy, made us alive with Christ even when we were dead in transgressions—it is by grace you have been saved." That text talks about the miracle of regeneration. Compare it to getting a new battery for your car. That car may look good on the outside, but without a battery, it's dead. It has the potential to get you places and do a lot of great things. But it's dead until it gets hooked up to a power source and gets a jolt—until it gets life breathed into it. Then it has something to offer. Then it comes alive.

The Scriptures tell us that when we come into this world we receive physical life. But our hearts stay cold and lifeless toward worship until the miracle of regeneration happens through what Christ did on the cross. The process begins when you say, "I'm tired of being dead. I'm tired of being cold and unmoved by God and by people. I want to be alive in my spirit. Alive on the inside." At that point, if you open your heart to Christ and ask, "Forgive me and make me come alive through what You did on the cross," He will. You will be regenerated, and your heart will change. And God will put to your credit Jesus' ten thousand consecutive spiritual free throws. That's what it means to have a righteousness that exceeds that of the scribes and Pharisees. You are now righteous, worshipful, and loving to the core. Why? When Jesus Christ fills you with His power and presence, *your* core is really *His* core in you.

Putting Yourself in the Picture

Challenge group members to take time in the coming week and use part or all of this application section as an opportunity for continued growth.

FIXING BROKEN RELATIONSHIPS

MATTHEW 5:21–26

INTRODUCTION

This lesson focuses on the *urgent need* for restoration and healing in relationships. Fixing broken relationships was a high priority in Jesus' book! It should also be at the top of our priority list.

As you lead this study, understand how sensitive this area is for many people. Some of your group members will have a built-in resistance to the truth in this passage of Scripture. Why? Because they are nursing deep wounds and holding on to anger and bitterness. They may not want to restore broken relationships. They may not have a desire to invest the time and energy needed to fix their broken relationships.

You might even have to be honest and admit to God that you are reluctant to open yourself to the truth of this lesson. As you prepare for your group to meet, pray for each member by name. Pray also for yourself. Ask the Holy Spirit to soften each heart and open the eyes of each group member to see relationships that need healing.

THE BIG PICTURE

Take time to read this introduction with the group. There are suggestions for how this section of the study can be used in the beginning of the leader's section.

A WIDE ANGLE VIEW

Question One Included in the introduction are a number of the rules of etiquette that we all know: Be on time, don't distract others, and don't stand up and leave in the middle of things. These, and other unwritten rules, are commonly accepted by most people.

Have some fun telling stories about how you or others have broken these rules. These stories may end up being humorous or simply examples of how we can cross the line of etiquette if we're not careful. They may be about ourselves or how others have crossed the line and how we responded to their rudeness.

To get the ball rolling, you may want to share this brief story from my own experience.

I was late for a Bears game one time. I had to crawl in the middle of a seating section. Wouldn't you know it, I had to get past one of those guys who's noticeably proud of his LARGE beer belly. I didn't know how I was going to get around this guy, because he wanted me to know he was mad that I was late. He just kind of smiled at me sarcastically with his belly hanging out there. I didn't know if I should limbo under it or climb over it. I'll tell you what, I'm going to show up on time next game!

Read Snapshot "Etiquette in the First Century" before Question 2

A BIBLICAL PORTRAIT

Read Matthew 5:21–26

Question Two Jesus makes some clear parallels between the damage and destruction of broken relationships and the sin of murder. Both of these destroy the lives of others and ourselves. With these words Jesus is saying, "Some of you people are so religious. You're breaking your arm patting yourself on your back because you have never murdered anybody. You think that because there are no bloodstains on your hands, you own a loving heart. You think you meet the kingdom's standard for relationships, but I say that some of you who have clean hands also have blood spattered all over the inside of your life. You are not loving at all toward people."

Jesus wants His followers to understand the seriousness of broken relationships and the grave consequences of letting these relationships go unchecked.

SHARPENING THE FOCUS

Read Snapshot "Which Boat Are You In?" before Question 3

Question Four The analogy of a family in a boat will help group members see how unresolved anger destroys our relationships with others as well as with God. Jesus taught that in His kingdom we need to be thinking of Christianity as a kind of family system. The Father is in the center of the boat and the brothers and sisters in various places around the boat. The desire of the Father is that the brothers and sisters in the boat would relate to Him warmly and to each other with hearts of love and grace. Because, if they do, what happens in the boat is wonderful. The joy of the relationships is multiplied. There is a life-giving atmosphere all around the boat. The aroma is so sweet that people on the shore crowd down by the beach. They wish they could go out and spend time in that boat because there's love in that boat. It's flowing all over the place.

On the other hand, some of us know very well that a boat is a terrible place to be if love breaks down. It's a confined space. Pretty soon you can smell it in the air . . . those faint traces of spoiled trust and rancid loyalties. You hear whispers of hurtful information being spread around the boat. Pretty soon sides are forming, accusations are being made and defended, and voices are becoming shrill and hostile.

We all know the painful truth. Unresolved anger destroys our relationships with others and eventually begins to spoil our relationship with the Father. This is why it is so important to deal with these broken relationships and deal with them now.

Question Five Allow group members to discuss some of their own experiences with broken relationships, including the results. You may be surprised at how severe some of the consequences are.

Realize some of these stories might be very recent and even part of your group members' experiences at this time. Listen closely to what they share, and commit yourself to pray for areas of pain and struggle in their lives or the lives of those they care about.

Question Six When we hold bitterness and anger in our hearts, they poison our relationships with others and with God. This, in turn, compromises our ability to communicate Christ to those who don't know the Savior. If they see that our faith does not lead to healing and wholeness, they will begin to question the power and purpose of the God we follow. When our hearts are ruled by unresolved anger and conflict in relationships, the light of our witness begins to burn dimmer and dimmer.

Read Snapshot "Critical Care" before Question 7

Questions Seven & Eight Part of the reason Jesus is advocating immediate action is that a breakdown of love is like a ruptured appendix. Once the rupture occurs, toxins spread quickly throughout a person's insides. Before you know it, someone is poisoned by hostility and resentment. Jesus knows how we're wired. He knows that we can be in a great relationship one day and then if something breaks, it can take less than twenty-four hours for the relationship to come apart.

It can happen that fast! This is why Jesus says speed is of the essence. Don't even chance waiting another thirty minutes until the service ends. Jesus uses a legal metaphor. He says if someone is going to sue you, you're better off trying to get together and settle out of court. If you go to court and start paying attorney's fees and you get all tied up in the judicial system, it's only going to make matters worse. Speed is of the essence. Settle it fast. This counsel corresponds to the wisdom of Ephesians 4:26 where Paul says, "Do not let the sun go down while you are still angry." Don't wait another twelve hours and give the toxins that much of a head start in your system. Take drastic action, because our witness to the world hangs in the balance and because our relationship to God will be encumbered if we don't. The thirty minutes we wait might be absolutely critical.

Question Nine The Bible says sometimes you will try to reconcile with someone and he or she will slam the door. The individual will want to keep fighting. At that time, we need to remember the words of Romans 12:18: "If it is possible, as far as it depends on you, live at peace with everyone." You have done your part. You can't control what happens on the other side.

You can still pray for the other person and seek healing whenever possible, but you can't force reconciliation if the person doesn't want a restored relationship. Your primary concern needs to be seeking peace and healing whenever possible. You do your part.

Question Ten There is no magic wand or simple formula for fixing broken relationships: Every relationship is unique; every relational breakdown is different and layered and complex; the players in the game are different; how long the toxins have had to poison the system varies. Because of these differences, I have found that sure-fire formulas are not worth much. However, there are some overarching principles from Scripture and from some personal experiences that might be helpful.

First, when you try to fix a broken relationship, your attitude is very important. When you walk in the room to meet the person with whom you have been in conflict, your demeanor will make a big difference in the reconciliation attempt. If you come in the room with a spirit of power, intimidation, self-righteousness, or arrogance, the other person will smell that a mile away. Trust me, it will not help the process.

But, if you walk into a room to reconcile with someone and your demeanor is gracious and gentle, you will build bridges rather than tear them down. Pray for humility and a heart filled with grace. Remember the forgiveness and patience God has given freely to you. Enter the room with the right attitude.

Second, when it's time to talk, your clear statement of intention really matters. One example would be, "Bob, I think we both know things have gone sour between us, but I really didn't come here to go toe-to-toe on everything we disagree about. What I want to say is that I would really like to reestablish our relationship, even if we can't agree on some things." That's a far cry from, "Look, Bob, we've got some problems, so let's get out the list, the jackhammers, and the boxing gloves. Let's find out who's wrong and who's right. Let's determine who's the loser and who's the winner in this deal." That approach rarely leads to reconciliation.

Third, forgiveness is awfully important. This doesn't mean tapping your foot until the other person apologizes. It means going in and owning your part of the breakdown very early in the talk, quietly and humbly asking to be forgiven. It's taken me years to get this, but I now understand that I own a part of almost every relational breakdown that occurs in my life.

PUTTING YOURSELF IN THE PICTURE

Challenge group members to take time in the coming week to use part or all of this application section as an opportunity for continued growth.

LOOKING, LUSTING, OR LOVING?

MATTHEW 5:27–30

INTRODUCTION

This lesson focuses on the human tendency to lust. Jesus approaches this topic head on when He challenges people to realize that sexual sin does not require skin-to-skin contact. We can dishonor God and sin sexually with our imaginations and in our thoughts. The truth is, the temptation to lust is ever present, and many people today don't realize the danger of entering into lusting. We live in a lust-filled culture that often encourages this practice and even counts on it to sell products and increase ratings on TV shows and in movies. This study addresses the topic from Jesus' point of view and calls us to live pure lives in our actions as well as our minds.

THE BIG PICTURE

Take time to read this introduction with the group. Be sure to pause and give people in your group time to use their imagination as they paint a picture in their mind of their favorite vacation place and the home where they grew up. There are suggestions for how this section of the study can be used in the beginning of the leader's section.

A BIBLICAL PORTRAIT

Read Matthew 5:27–30

Question Three There's a dark side to our ability to imagine. If you haven't already guessed what it is, you lack imagination! The shadow side of being able to imagine something is that we also have the ability to imagine ourselves in God-dishonoring, self-destructive scenarios. And we can do that and still look good on the outside. Nobody around us even knows what's going on in our heart and mind.

Against the backdrop of talking about the power of human imagination, Jesus fearlessly forged ahead into the arena of human sexuality. Without breaking stride, Jesus marched into this forbidden zone and says, "Lots of you are feeling really righteous because you've never committed adultery. But some of you have been hopping from bed to bed in your heart and in your mind." Jesus wanted everyone to know that in His kingdom, lust of the heart is to be seen as a major problem. Jesus alerted the people to the fact that some of them were regularly commissioning their imaginations to crank out sexually explicit motion pictures *starring themselves!* Jesus was saying to that crowd the very same things He wants to say to us today: "Take this issue of lust very seriously! What happens in your mind has serious consequences on how you live your life!"

I talked to a guy some time ago who hates his job. More specifically, he hates his boss. He was telling me that he relives a certain scenario in his mind. Sometimes he thinks about mustering up the courage to go into his boss's office, grab him by the lapels, scream obscenities at him, and then hang him on the chandelier of his big office. I said, "Do you really think that kind of stuff?" And he said, "I've thought it in my head a hundred times." He said, "You know, it makes me feel good. I can get even with my boss without losing my job." But he said, "It's only a mind game. And nobody knows about it."

We can play those kinds of dishonoring mind games, and no one knows, because we can do it without moving a muscle, without breaking a facial expression, without tipping our hand to what's happening in our heart. The truth is, we can commission our imagination to work in dishonorable and destructive ways, or we can commission our imagination to work in honorable and uplifting ways. Our imagination can be driven by anger, lust, and jealousy. It can also be guided by compassion, love, and creativity. When it is driven by negative attitudes, it can become a monster. When our imagination is directed by things that are pleasing to God, it is a wonderful gift.

Jesus wants us to know that there is more then one way to commit sexual sin. You can commit adultery without clothes on in a motel room, or you can commit adultery fully clothed in your living room, at work, or right in the middle of a church service. Both forms of adultery, physical and mental, emanate from the same self-seeking, lustful heart. Jesus says, "In My kingdom, I'm looking for people whose hearts are loving to the core, not lustful to the core. I'm looking for hearts that are sexually pure."

SHARPENING THE FOCUS

Read Snapshot "A Broad Spectrum" before Question 4

Question Four This is an opportunity to allow for a free exchange of ideas. As you discuss cultural norms in this area, you could get a wide variety of perspectives. The goal is not to force a consensus, but to allow group members to express their perspective on all three levels.

Most groups will not be ready to discuss this question out loud. Provide a time for silent reflection and allow each person to honestly assess where they are on this continuum. If you are meeting with a group of all men or all women who are comfortable with one another and have established a clear pattern of confidentiality, you may want to ask them if they would like to respond to this question as a group. However, this is certainly not an area where you want to force a response . . . particularly in a mixed group with both men and women.

Read Snapshot "Image Bearers" before Question 5

Read Snapshot "Living in a Sin-stained World" before Question 6

Read Snapshot "When Lust Runs Wild" before Question 7

Question Seven Your understanding of how this continuum works is vital to the health of your spiritual life. It's also critical to the health of your relating patterns. If you find yourself in the middle or down on the lust side of the continuum, there is reason for huge concern and for actions that will release you from the grip of a lust-filled life.

I want to give you two reasons why the Scriptures say you're in trouble if you live on the lust end of the spectrum. First, lust always violates the law of love. Jesus says in John 13:35, "By this all men will know that you are my disciples, if you love one another." When people outside the kingdom of God see the depth and the genuineness of our love for each other, brother-to-brother, sister-to-sister, men-to-women, women-to-men they look on and say, "Only God could produce a love like that." Love is the kingdom trump card.

Love, in the context of male/female relationships, is defined in Scripture as fully-dimensional males entering into friendship community with fully-dimensional females. Whole men entering into friendship and community with women holistically. Anything other than that violates the law of love. Lust, by its very nature, is reductionary. It tends to be visceral and one dimensional. Whenever we start reducing people from being whole image bearers to mere bodies to gratify our sexual desires physically or in our own minds, Jesus says that's a violation of the law of love. When we become reductionary and think mostly of bodies instead of whole people, we become users of each other instead of servants.

Sometimes this is hard for men to understand. Women seem to have a pretty good sense of the awfulness of feeling used in a sexual way. I have had women tell me that they were somewhere shopping and someone made a sexual comment to them. They have told me how disgusting they felt at that moment. When you ask those women, "Was there any part of that remark that was flattering to you and felt like a compliment?" most of the time, if it was a clearly sexual remark, the woman will respond and say, "It felt filthy. It felt awful. It made me just feel like an animal or an object." There's no love in lust-filled comments, actions, or daydreams. At that point the person is not trying to enter into community with someone who is a fully-dimensional creature. They want to grab just the physical/sexual side of them, use it up, and discard it. This violates the law of love.

A second reason to be very concerned about lust is that it tends to be progressive in nature. By that I mean it tends to require more and more stimulation to achieve the same measure of fleeting pleasure. I received this anonymous letter some time ago.

> Dear Bill,
>
> I'm an emotional invalid. Lust is eating me up. It paralyzes my spiritual life. It perverts my view of women. It distorts my social life. It wreaks havoc in my emotional stability. It destroys any possibility of God using me in the church. But I can't stop it. Recently, I've become addicted to pornography, which has simply intensified the problem. And the sad part is that I know that lust and pornography promise everything and produce nothing. But I still just can't seem to stop.

Now, that is someone who probably started in the middle of the continuum and walked a little bit toward lust, then a little bit more, and then moved so far into lust that it became the defining value in his life, not God or loving relationships. And he can't stop it.

Lust has that kind of addictive power. Lust is every bit as addictive as alcohol and drugs. Life starts to revolve around it. It is a ruthless taskmaster. The letter said it well. It promises everything and delivers nothing. And at the end, it will spit you out. It will call you a fool. Sometimes we just have to remind ourselves what lust really is. It's a relationship-busting, love-diminishing, self-destructive, dead-end deal. People who lust a lot tend to drift away from the understanding and the design for what the gift of sexuality is really all about. Pretty soon sex is no longer a good gift of God given to married couples for the intimate expression of love in the context of a healthy marriage. Pretty soon, if you lust enough, sex becomes a mental or physical athletic endeavor with nameless bodies and loveless souls that leave the lustful man or woman a little emptier and a little lonelier after each go-around. Inject into that the fear of sexually transmitted diseases and unwanted pregnancies, and you have a nightmare on your hands. That's the current condition in our society: it's a sexual nightmare.

Question Eight Jesus says that if you want to move away from lust and toward God's ideal, it's going to take some drastic steps. "If your right eye makes you stumble, tear it out. If your right hand makes you stumble, cut it off. It's better to go into heaven missing a few body parts then to be complete with a body and wind up in hell," he says. Is Jesus really suggesting physical mutilation? Absolutely not! He is seeking to paint a clear and vivid picture in our minds. He wants us to know just how serious this issue of lust really is. Jesus is saying that we need to starve whatever feeds our lust. How do you shut off a diesel engine? You starve its fuel supply. How do you move out of lust? Starve whatever it is that supplies your lustful thoughts. If your fuel for lust is the images in magazines, videos, movies, television, or certain persons or practices, shut off that supply. Jesus is saying, "If it's images that feed your lust, go blind to those images. If your arm is reaching for the car keys to drive you to a place that feeds your lust, respond as an amputee. If your feet are trying to take you to a lust-feeding facility, go lame." Jesus wants us to take dramatic steps to move away from lust and toward God's ideal for human relationships. Let's expand on those three steps.

First, *cut off the supply of whatever encourages lust in your life*. Some people in your group will want someone to spell it out for them. "Which movies are appropriate and which aren't? Which videos are okay? Which places can we go and where can't we go? Let's take all the mystery out of it." We can't do that. Why? Because Jesus didn't do it. Jesus just gave the overarching principle. Go blind or lame to whatever feeds your lust. Shut off the fuel supply to whatever feeds your lusts. And let us not forget

different stimuli excite different people in different ways. I
don't know what feeds your lust and you don't know what
feeds mine. So what we have to do is just agree and obey Jesus'
basic principle. Whatever it is for us . . . starve it!

I remember speaking at a conference a couple of years ago at a
resort located by an ocean. I gave a couple of talks and then I
mentioned to the leader of the conference that I was going to
go take a walk on the beach to clear my head before I came
back and gave the final talk. He looked at me with a disturbed
expression and said, "You're going to go down there where all
those half-naked women are lying seductively in the sand
soaking up suntan lotion and drinking beer?" And I thought,
"I was just going to look at some boats." I didn't really have
anything sexual in mind. I just wanted to go down and see if
there were any race boats out. What he communicated to me
was that if he were to walk down to that beach, he might
have a problem lusting. Let's not start making arbitrary rules
for all of us and become overly legalistic. The main thing is
that we all have to learn to starve whatever feeds our lust.

A second way to move from lust toward the ideal way of
relating is to *fill your mind with constructive images and information.* In case you haven't learned yet, it's almost impossible to
break a well-established pattern of thought by trying to just
stop it. Have you ever had someone do that to you? Sometimes Christian leaders do. They say, "As far as this lust thing
goes—just stop thinking those thoughts." Did you ever say,
"I'm never going to think about that again"? You lock it into
your mind. But now you've just tuned your mind into the
very thing you did not want to think about anymore.

The Bible takes another approach. In Philippians 4:8 we are
told to displace lustful thoughts with "whatever is true, whatever is noble, whatever is right, whatever is pure, whatever is
lovely, whatever is admirable." Be intentional about putting
good thoughts into your mind, and they will slowly and sure-
ly displace the lustful thoughts occupied there. Put better stuff
in there, and then the bad stuff will go to the side and leak out.
What you put in your mind determines, to a large extent, who
you are and what you will become. If you put a bunch of
garbage into your mind, your thought life will be trashy. If
you fill your mind with a better product, you will tend to
think with a higher degree of purity.

Awhile back I was driving through downtown Chicago and I
happened to be listening to a worship tape that launched me
into community with God. In the quietness of that moment I

really felt close to God and I felt His love just flowing over me. While I was stopped at a red light, many people were crossing in front of me, and as I watched them I just wanted to reach out and encourage every one of them and say, "You matter to God. God loves you."

Then I heard a low, resonating bounce. I thought, "Is a train coming?" No, it wasn't a train; it was a car with about a $5,000 sound system. It had woofers that were pounding out hostile, aggressive-sounding music. The car pulled up next to me with five guys in it, windows down, stereo turned up to ten and blasting this hostile kind of music. Here I am listening to praise music. When I looked over at those guys and my eyes met theirs, I realized we were in totally different places. The music I was listening to was leading me to encourage people. The music they were listening to, from what I observed, made them hostile. I realized that what we were listening to was powerfully impacting our view of human relationships.

What you intentionally put into your mind, the quality of material, the books you read, the magazines you subscribe to, the music you listen to, the places you go, what you expose yourself to, either fills your mind with thoughts that move you toward the loving end of the continuum or fills your mind with thoughts that keep you down at the dead-end-street side of the lust-filled continuum. You make the choice.

Third, *build healthy, integrity-filled relationships that honor God.* The Scriptures call us to recommit ourselves to building and nurturing truly loving relationships. Here's how it works. Love is the kingdom trump card. As we learn to build truly loving relationships with one another, the Holy Spirit will help us want to enter community in holistic ways with each other. We'll want to get to know each other intellectually, emotionally, relationally. We'll appreciate each other's physical/sexual selves, but we will not cross biblical boundaries and violate sexual rules with regard to relating to each other as whole people.

The more you enter into community in loving ways with men and women, the more likely you are to continue that pattern when you're in what could be a tempting situation. I have learned this lesson on many occasions, but one comes to mind that might be helpful. I was coming back from out of town and I was on a commercial airliner. I was playing the "who's going to sit next to me" game. Did you ever play it? I was on the aisle about halfway down in the economy class section. I kept looking down the aisle, wondering who would come and sit in the seat right next to me and be there for the duration of the flight. You know, sometimes you think, "No. No, please." Other times you want to stand up and say, "Here's your seat."

Anyway, it just so happened that nobody filled the seats next to me. However, a very lovely young woman sat directly across the aisle from me. I'll use a biblical expression to tell you how lovely she was: She was beautiful in face and form. (If you say it that way, it's okay. That's the way a pastor says it!) To be honest, I noticed the fact that she was beautiful in face and form and there was a little energy generated. Midway through the flight she asked me for something to read. We were soon engaged in a conversation. In just about a ten-to-fifteen minute period of time, I learned that she was in a dead-end relationship with a boyfriend who was an alcoholic and treated her abusively. She had some friends who had failed her, so she was disappointed relationally. She was spiritually confused. Didn't have a clue about where she was headed, but wanted to find some life direction.

What I'm describing to you is that I entered into a holistic conversation with her. After we deplaned and she headed one way for a connecting flight and I went home, I reflected as I was walking to the baggage claim area. I said, "I really like the way that I related to her. I really do." That was not a lust-filled encounter. She did not become just a pretty face and form. She was a full image bearer of God with thoughts and feelings. She became a person who was one prayer away from becoming an adopted daughter of the Father. She became someone for me to serve and to pray for, not someone to mentally seduce and use. I really felt satisfied with the way the encounter unfolded. I said, "That's what I want to be." I don't want to be a lust-filled man. I don't even want to be in the middle of the continuum. I want to be someone who relates to men and women in a holistically healthy, true, loving way.

At this point I feel it is important to add a fourth way to move from the lust-controlled heart of the continuum to the God-pleasing end: *Seek professional help if you are deep into sexual sin and can't seem to get out on your own.*

Some members of your group might be stuck in lust in a very extreme way, and it's tearing them apart. There's probably an underlying reason why they are that far into lust. I would urge you to help them find a Christian counselor or pastor with whom they can honestly relate how lust has them by the throat and is ruining their life. I have found that people who take the courageous step to go to a Christian counselor discover that, in almost every case, the secret reason why they are that far into lust can be identified and processed and they can be liberated in ways they never thought possible.

Question Nine Remember that many members may be feeling guilty about their past. If you can acknowledge this fact, you may take some pressure off them. Remind members how total the forgiveness of Christ is. Focus on the future and less on the past.

PUTTING YOURSELF IN THE PICTURE

Challenge group members to take time in the coming week and use part or all of this application section as an opportunity for continued growth.

An Audience of One

Matthew 6:1–18

Introduction

We live in a world where performance is valued and important. So much of what we do is seen, evaluated, graded, and compensated. In the midst of a performance-centered world, Christ followers are called to live to an audience of One. We are not to live our lives for people, but for Jesus alone. When we do this, we will gain great eternal rewards. When we live to please others, we will get our earthly reward and applause, but we will miss the heavenly reward. We need to learn the secret of living our whole lives for God's glory.

The Big Picture

Take time to read this introduction with the group. There are suggestions for how this can be done in the beginning of this leader's section.

A Biblical Portrait

Read Matthew 6:1–18

Sharpening the Focus

Read Snapshot "A Serious Warning" before Question 3

Questions Three & Four Jesus does something interesting in Matthew 6:1–18. He explains what I call the "kingdom law of compensation." It works a little bit like compensation in the marketplace. For instance, He might use the following analogy if He were teaching today: If you spend a forty-hour work week plugging away at IBM, don't go over to Hewlett Packard and expect them to pay you when payday comes. You didn't work for them! You worked for IBM. If you sell Reebok shoes for a living, and you're setting all kinds of records, you will expect to be paid by Reebok. You don't expect a paycheck from Nike. You should only expect to be compensated by the one you're working for.

Here's the kingdom law of compensation: Jesus wants us to know that if the primary reason we do "spiritual" or "Christian" things, attend Christian meetings, and show up in church is to please our spouse, kids, date, pastor, or elders, then we have already received our reward. It's not a nasty, awful, shameful thing. But if we do it to please them, their pleasure is our reward. Don't expect anything more than that. You're getting paid from the one you're working for. If that's who you're trying to please, you pleased them. Done deal. But Jesus says the tragedy is that other people's approval isn't worth it. Applause is fickle and fleeting. And what's even worse is that you'll miss the reward your heart yearns for . . . affirmation from your Father in heaven. You don't want to miss His rewards. You don't want to miss His compensations. They're rich. They satisfy the soul.

If the primary reason you give money to Christian causes is so you can make sure your name is written down in the church record somewhere, you have your compensation. If you're giving money because you don't want to be embarrassed about not putting something in the plate, when you get a little pat on the back from somebody who notices, that's all you're going to get. But if you give money to kingdom causes because you are overwhelmed with the love of God and you're grateful for the way Jesus has changed your heart, forgiven your past, and extended grace to you, if you are doing it for Him, Jesus says, "Then your Father, who sees what is done in secret, will reward you" (Matt. 6:4).

If the primary reason you pray is because you're training little kids at home and you've got to pray for their sake, you're missing the point. If you're going to a restaurant with some other Christians and you've got to pray to keep up appearances, your appearance is your reward. Jesus says when that prayer is over and someone says, "Nice prayer," that's all you get. But if you pray because you want to talk to the God who loves you, your reward is great. When you want to have a conversation with Him and tell Him how you feel, He loves it. If you're praying to the Father because of your love for Him and your relationship with Him, then Jesus says "Your Father, who sees what is done in secret, will reward you."

In Matthew 7:22–23, Jesus says a lot of people are going to stand before the holy God on the Day of Reckoning and be proud of their church attendance, giving record, prayer meeting attendance, and service projects, and to their horror, they're going to hear God the Father say, "I never knew you. Away from me, you evildoers!" God says, "You weren't doing all that stuff for Me. You did it for the applause of people. You did it for your spouse, your parents, your pastor, your friend. You did it to fit into a group. You did it to feel less lonely. You did it for a lot of reasons. You just didn't do it primarily for Me, so depart from Me." Jesus wants to spare us from that. We matter too much for Him not to warn us of that possible tragedy. Out of love He stops His listeners and says, "Before we go any further let's take a motivation check. Why are you doing the things you do?" The answer to this question has eternal implications.

Read Snapshot "The Secrecy Test" before Question 5

Question Five The secrecy test exposes motivations. It tends to clarify what you're doing for others and what you're doing out of a loving response to God. This secrecy test determines who is impressing others and who is seeking to please an audience of One.

As you talk about the motives for displaying religious actions in front of others, discussion may get a little intense. The fact is, many prayers and acts of service and giving are motivated by a desire to please people. Tender nerves may be touched in this discussion. However, uncovering and identifying the wrong motives is essential if there is going to be a change in our hearts. You may have to lead the way as the leader, exposing some of your own weaknesses.

**Read Snapshot "An Essential Encounter"
before Question 6**

Question Six A biblical example will help clarify this point. In the New Testament there is a man named Saul. Later he's called the apostle Paul. He is intensely religious. He's a competitive guy. He's trying to impress all of his friends (especially his teachers in religion) with his knowledge, his purity, and most of all, his zeal. He wants to be first in his spiritual class, and in time Saul obtains his goal. There is just one problem, he's never met God.

One day he gets on his horse and rides to a city called Damascus. God says, "I'm going to meet this guy." (The story is written in Acts 9:1–19.) As Saul travels down the road, a bright light shines. There's a thunderous voice from heaven. He falls off his horse, collapses in the dust, and the first thing God does is remove his eyesight. There's a very important reason, I think, why God removed Saul's eyesight temporarily. Saul had lived his whole religious life looking around, making sure he was getting approving glances and smiles from people. So

God says, "Your eyesight has to go. I don't want you getting clues or cues from any human being anymore. You've got to get to know Me—God."

In the darkness God introduced Himself to Saul. It was as if God said, "I sent My Son Jesus to pay for your sins. I love you, Saul. You don't have to keep achieving and performing and doing all these drills. You just have to give Me your heart. We've got to get into a relationship." You know what happened? That day on the Damascus road, and shortly thereafter, Saul repented of all of the playacting and all the spiritual pretending. He repented of all the hoop jumping and people-pleasing, and he gave his life to Christ. Almost overnight his addiction to men's applause was broken. He became a humble servant for an audience of One.

Do you want to know the first question Paul asked God after his true conversion? He said, "Lord, what would You have me do?" He had never asked a question like that before. It was always what do the teachers want me to do? What do the rabbis want me to do? What do my buddies want me to do? What does this person want time to do? Now he's asking only one question, "Lord, what would You have me do?"

When I meet people I can usually tell in ten to fifteen minutes if they're socialized Christians who are just kind of going through the motions to please somebody or if they've had an encounter with the true God who has fundamentally changed their heart. I can tell and so can most of you.

As Christ followers we will have many encounters with God as we grow in our faith. They are not always earth-shattering, and there is not often thunder and a heavenly voice. Often it's quieter than that. But if you've ever had an encounter with God, you'll never forget it.

I had an encounter with God once when I traveled to a city to give a specific message. After a few minutes of praying, I got the sense from the Holy Spirit that He didn't want me to give that talk and I panicked. It was the only talk I had brought and I'm not good at making them up on the spot, so I kept praying and said, "Now, I'm willing to do Plan B, but You'd better reveal it to me." I started reading the Bible and I stumbled across a text that I had been studying in my private devotional life. It was as if God said, "Teach from this text." I took the phone pad on the night stand at the hotel and wrote down some thoughts.

I went to the place scared stiff. There was a big group gathered. I walked up and started giving this completely new talk. About five minutes into it I felt so strongly the presence of God in my life that I said things I didn't know I was capable of saying. I had insights that I didn't think I knew. And I did something that I don't ever recall having done after giving a talk. I asked the host of the talk, "Could you send me a tape of that?" Now, you've got to understand that I never listen to my tapes. If you want to torture me, put a tape of one of my talks into a recorder and make me listen to it. But that one was such a remarkable experience that I just wanted to relive it again through the tape.

Do you know what I did when I went back to my hotel room that night? I fell on my knees right by the bed and made a private pact again with God. I don't know about you, but every time I have an encounter with God that's important, I make a new pact. I prayed, "God, after a meeting like this, You are so real to me and Your love is so strong in my life that I want to underscore my intention to orient all of my life around You, to honor You, to worship You, to do Your bidding, to make my life count for Your purposes. That's the intention of my heart again today."

Next time you have an experience with God, be sure to commit your whole heart to serve only Him, to orient your whole life around pleasing only Him. It might be this week. It might be happening right now. If you're open to those kinds of encounters, when God shows up and you have one of those experiences with Him, it will be the inclination of your heart to let God know that you don't want to waste your life trying to gain the approval of people. Let God know that you want to spend all of your life living only for His approval and applause.

Question Seven We need to learn how to open ourselves up to these kinds of encounters. God loves them. One text that proves this is James 4:8: "Come near to God and he will come near to you." The idea is that when you reach out your hand, He'll touch it. Draw near to God. He wants to make connections with you. It's His heart. But what happens when you have some of these encounters, dramatic or not so dramatic? Guess what happens over time? You make a decision to become decidedly less public about your acts of service. You want to become a secret giver, a secret prayer, a secret faster, and a secret servant because you remember this truth: "Your Father, who sees what is done in secret, will reward you."

As you go into the coming week, you might bump into someone who is carrying a lot of sorrow. It is written all over her face. Let's say the Spirit of God prompts you to stop and talk with her or just put your arm on her shoulder for a second and say, "I don't know what's going on, but you matter to God and you matter to me. I just wanted you to know." You might find yourself praying for her every day for the whole week. No one but God hears your prayer, but you care so much that you lift her up to the Father who hears your prayer in secret. The Father who sees in secret knows what you did. The Father saw that loving thing and heard those loving words. And the Scripture says, "He will reward you."

PUTTING YOURSELF IN THE PICTURE

Challenge group members to take time in the coming week to use part or all of this application section as an opportunity for continued growth.

WHY WORRY?

MATTHEW 6:25—34

INTRODUCTION

In this portion of the Sermon on the Mount, Jesus tackles the very serious problem of worry. We live in a worry-filled age and the message of Jesus speaks as loudly today as it did to the crowd gathered on the mountainside almost two thousand years ago. The message for Christ's followers is clear: Don't worry about tomorrow but throw yourself into full devotion to the Father today. When we seek first His desires and plan, He promises to take care of the rest.

THE BIG PICTURE

Take time to read this introduction with the group. There are suggestions for how this can be done in the beginning of the leader's section.

A WIDE ANGLE VIEW

Question One Allow time for open communication of various fears and anxieties. These might range from something as small as a fear of spiders to a deep and paralyzing fear of death. The dialogue could stay on the surface or go very deep if group members begin communicating genuine and deep fears and anxieties. Again, you as leader may need to set the pace and tone of the discussion.

A BIBLICAL PORTRAIT

Read Matthew 6:25–34

Question Two The first question in this section is answered on several different levels. As Jesus continued speaking, He gave very specific reasons why we can live without having worry dominate our lives. Allow group members to dig into the passage and seek to discover Jesus' answers together before you move into the rest of the study. The following side notes will bring greater clarity, but allow time to let the Spirit speak through the text before reading the Snapshots.

There is great power in personal testimonies. Most, if not all, of the members of your group have experienced times when

God has given them a supernatural peace and calm in the midst of anxiety-filled circumstances. Allow time for group members to tell their stories. This will set the tone for the rest of the study.

SHARPENING THE FOCUS

Read Snapshot "You're More Than Just a Body" before Question 3

Question Three In this passage Jesus gives an argument for trust based on how He has made us. His reasoning goes like this: God has gone to enormous trouble to create, love, redeem, and renew your inner person. Therefore, it would make no sense for Him to neglect you. The details of life such as food, drink, shelter, and clothing all matter to God. In comparison to your inner person, they are just trivia. Small potatoes. No-problem stuff.

Can you imagine a world-class heart surgeon spending twelve hours doing a meticulous heart transplant operation on a person and sewing him up, only to neglect to order a bed, blankets, food, and drink in post-op care? Would a good surgeon do this surgery and then let his or her patient die of starvation two weeks later? It would never happen! That's the spirit of what Jesus is saying. He's saying, "God has seen to the really important stuff inside of you. The Great Physician who did that transforming work in your heart will see to it that your daily food and clothing needs are met."

Question Four Jesus says, "Look at the birds of the air; they do not sow or reap or store away in barns, and yet your heavenly Father feeds them." And here's the key point: "Are you not much more valuable then they?" Human beings are more valuable than birds. I know this fact is widely debated these days by spotted owl lovers, but listen to Jesus' argument. He says, "When was the last time you were walking out in nature and you saw a bird in full flight run out of fuel and crash to the ground?" The fact is, birds tend to do fine with regard to fuel, food, and drink. Jesus wants us to realize that birds don't stockpile. They don't steal or kill for food. They find food for the day and they trust that there will be food tomorrow. Jesus is drawing our attention to the fact that His Father does a pretty good job of taking care of little birds, as well as the entire ecosystem. Even birds matter to Him.

And then comes the punch line, "You matter far more than any bird." Jesus is saying, "Would you relax? Take the plunge

into full devotion to My Father and then trust Me for the rest."
He is not giving license to be careless and foolish with our
money management, but He *is* inviting us to stop fretting
about the future. Birds are wonderful and they're valuable,
but they're not image bearers of God the Father. Birds are
amazing little creatures, but God wouldn't have spilled the
blood of His only Son for them. He would only do that for
people like you and me. Because we matter far more than
birds. The truth is . . . we matter deeply to God!

There are many powerful examples of how God provides for
His creation. As your group members tell stories of how they
have seen God care for His creation, seek to help them hear
the promise of Jesus to care for them far more than He cares
for the birds of the air.

Read Snapshot "Worry Does Not Change Things" before Question 5

Question Five I remember some years ago sitting next to a
woman on a very turbulent, late-night commercial flight. She
was very nervous and manifested some of the telltale signs of
acute anxiety. Hand wringing, looking around nervously, and
gasping for breath were a few of the clues that this woman
was worried. I had just given five or six talks that day and I
was exhausted. In spite of the lightning, thunder, and the air
pockets, I was dozing. And it became apparent to me when I
woke up and looked over at this woman that she was pretty
irritated that I was able to doze off during the storm.

It was as if she were saying, "You're not pulling your share of
the worry duty here. We all need to worry together if we're
ever going to get home." I remember thinking to myself,
"Doesn't she know that heart-pounding, hand-wringing,
shirt-soaking anxiety has never affected the performance of a
plane or pilot?" The fact is, you can't stop an electrical storm
or turbulence by worrying. You also can't get the pilot to
make a smooth landing just by being anxious.

I've learned over the years that when I am in an anxiety-filled
situation, I need to trust completely in God's power to provide and sustain. The words to a praise song come to mind,
"My life is in Your hands. What better place to be?"

I'm not better or more courageous than anybody else. But I
have come to understand and believe that worry doesn't
accomplish anything constructive. Why not take the energy
that gives rise to worry and convert it into a simple, trust-filled
prayer, "My life is in Your hands."

Read Snapshot "Humans Last Longer Than Flowers" before Question 6

Question Six I think Jesus is making two points here. The first is obvious. The second is a little more subtle. First, Jesus wants us to know that if God dresses lilies so beautifully, which only live for a brief season, how much more will He see to the clothing needs of His children who can live many years here on earth and forever in eternity. It's an argument based on longevity and value.

I think Jesus was saying that God the Father enjoys an occasional fashion-designing challenge with flowers and with people. I know some people take this verse and say God is basically against fashion. He's saying not to worry about clothes; they're not important. I don't think that's what the passage is suggesting. I think we get a unique glimpse of God at work in this text. Personally, I don't think God minded His challenge of dressing the lily. I don't think He minds the challenge of dressing the rose or the carnation, the daisy or the orchid. I think maybe He even enjoyed winning the fashion competition against the likes of Solomon.

I have found it to be true in my life that when I have set my heart and affections on loving God first and carrying out His purposes, God has provided generously for me and my family each step of the way.

Early in the ministry of Willow Creek my family lived on a very limited budget. The idea of going out and buying a new suit was almost unthinkable. However, God provided. A friend of mine had bought a new suit and had gained quite a bit of weight. He said, "I'll never fit in that suit again. Why don't you take it and start wearing it?" It was really something. A few years after that we started having children. A family came to our church and received Christ. They had a whole bunch of kids, and my kids' ages seemed to fit right in the hand-me-down sequence. The clothes would go from their kid to their next kid, to my kid, back to their next kid, back to my kid. Isn't that just like God?

I'm not saying that fashion is the top priority on God's agenda in the world today. Nor do I think God says to His children, "Get ready for burlap the rest of your life." I think He's a bigger God than that, and I think His creativity and His love of color and design even affects the way He promises to provide clothing for those who follow Him. And so, if you follow Christ fully and you take the plunge into full devotion, don't be surprised if God begins meeting your needs in marvelous ways. And if you're in a position to provide clothing for the poor, buy them good stuff. Dress them like God dressed the lily. Let Him work some miracles through you!

Question Seven In verses 31 and 32 Jesus says, "Do not worry, saying, 'What shall we eat?' or 'What shall we drink?' or 'What shall we wear?' For the pagans run after all these things, and your heavenly Father knows that you need them." Jesus says to take the dive into full devotion because Christ followers have a loving Father. You know, it makes perfect sense for people outside the family of God to fret and worry about their upcoming material needs. Because in a very real sense, they're on their own in this world. They've rejected God's fathership and lordship. They're living independent from Him. But Jesus turns to those who are followers of His Father and says, "But you are not orphans. You are not alone in this world. You have a Father, a heavenly Father, who loves you more than words can say." Jesus wants us to trust in Him to meet our needs.

Question Eight As you discuss these questions, realize that different people look at needs and wants in dramatically different ways. Don't try to create a legalistic list of absolute minimums for living. What you need to do is clarify that there are some things we really need and then there are lots of things we want. God's promise is to meet all of our needs. And when we really look at what He does for us, we realize that He also meets many of our wants.

I believe it breaks the heart of God when we stand looking into a full refrigerator and say, "There's nothing to eat," or stand looking into a closet filled with clothes and say, "I have nothing to wear." Too often we have all we need and a surplus on top of our needs. Yet, in our focus on what we want, we fail to see how much God has already provided. Sometimes we need to readjust how we see things . . . we need a new perspective.

Read Snapshot "God Keeps His Promises" before Question 9

PUTTING YOURSELF IN THE PICTURE

Challenge group members to take time in the coming week and use part or all of this application section as an opportunity for continued growth.

ADDITIONAL WILLOW CREEK RESOURCES

Small Group Resources

Coaching Life-Changing Small Group Leaders, by Bill Donahue and Greg Bowman
The Complete Book of Questions, by Garry Poole
The Connecting Church, by Randy Frazee
Leading Life-Changing Small Groups, by Bill Donahue and the Willow Creek Team
The Seven Deadly Sins of Small Group Ministry, by Bill Donahue and Russ Robinson
Walking the Small Group Tightrope, by Bill Donahue and Russ Robinson

Evangelism Resources

Becoming a Contagious Christian (book), by Bill Hybels and Mark Mittelberg
The Case for a Creator, by Lee Strobel
The Case for Christ, by Lee Strobel
The Case for Faith, by Lee Strobel
Seeker Small Groups, by Garry Poole
The Three Habits of Highly Contagious Christians, by Garry Poole

Spiritual Gifts and Ministry

Network Revised (training course), by Bruce Bugbee and Don Cousins
The Volunteer Revolution, by Bill Hybels
What You Do Best in the Body of Christ—Revised, by Bruce Bugbee

Marriage and Parenting

Fit to Be Tied, by Bill and Lynne Hybels
Surviving a Spiritual Mismatch in Marriage, by Lee and Leslie Strobel

Ministry Resources

An Hour on Sunday, by Nancy Beach
Building a Church of Small Groups, by Bill Donahue and Russ Robinson
The Heart of the Artist, by Rory Noland
Making Your Children's Ministry the Best Hour of Every Kid's Week, by Sue Miller and David Staal
Thriving as an Artist in the Church, by Rory Noland

Curriculum

An Ordinary Day with Jesus, by John Ortberg and Ruth Haley Barton
Becoming a Contagious Christian (kit), by Mark Mittelberg, Lee Strobel, and Bill Hybels
Good Sense Budget Course, by Dick Towner, John Tofilon, and the Willow Creek Team
If You Want to Walk on Water, You've Got to Get Out of the Boat, by John Ortberg with Stephen and Amanda Sorenson
The Life You've Always Wanted, by John Ortberg with Stephen and Amanda Sorenson
The Old Testament Challenge, by John Ortberg with Kevin and Sherry Harney, Mindy Caliguire, and Judson Poling

WILLOW
Willow Creek Association

Willow Creek Association
Vision, Training, Resources for Prevailing Churches

This resource was created to serve you and to help you build a local church that prevails. It is just one of many ministry tools that are part of the Willow Creek Resources® line, published by the Willow Creek Association together with Zondervan.

The Willow Creek Association (WCA) was created in 1992 to serve a rapidly growing number of churches from across the denominational spectrum that are committed to helping unchurched people become fully devoted followers of Christ. Membership in the WCA now numbers over 10,500 Member Churches worldwide from more than ninety denominations.

The Willow Creek Association links like-minded Christian leaders with each other and with strategic vision, training, and resources in order to help them build prevailing churches designed to reach their redemptive potential. Here are some of the ways the WCA does that.

- **A2: Building Prevailing Acts 2 Churches—Today**—an annual two-and-a-half day event, held at Willow Creek Community Church in South Barrington, Illinois, to explore strategies for building churches that reach out to seekers and build believers, and to discover new innovations and breakthroughs from Acts 2 churches around the country.

- **The Leadership Summit**—a once a year, two-and-a-half-day conference to envision and equip Christians with leadership gifts and responsibilities. Presented live at Willow Creek as well as via satellite broadcast to over one hundred locations across North America, this event is designed to increase the leadership effectiveness of pastors, ministry staff, volunteer church leaders, and Christians in the marketplace.

- **Ministry-Specific Conferences**—throughout each year the WCA hosts a variety of conferences and training events—both at Willow Creek's main campus and offsite, across the U.S., and around the world—targeting church leaders and volunteers in ministry-specific areas such as: evangelism, small groups, preaching and teaching, the arts, children, students, women, volunteers, stewardship, raising up resources, etc.

- **Willow Creek Resources®**—provides churches with trusted and field-tested ministry resources in such areas as leadership, evangelism, spiritual formation, spiritual gifts, small groups, stewardship, student ministry, children's ministry, the use of the arts-drama, media, contemporary music —and more.

- **WCA Member Benefits**—includes substantial discounts to WCA training events, a 20 percent discount on all Willow Creek Resources®, *Defining Moments* monthly audio journal for leaders, quarterly *Willow* magazine, access to a Members-Only section on WillowNet, monthly communications, and more. Member Churches also receive special discounts and premier services through WCA's growing number of ministry partners—Select Service Providers—and save an average of $500 annually depending on the level of engagement.

For specific information about WCA conferences, resources, membership, and other ministry services contact:

Willow Creek Association
P.O. Box 3188
Barrington, IL 60011-3188
Phone: 847-570-9812
Fax: 847-765-5046
www.willowcreek.com